INSTALL ELECTRICAL BREAKERS FOR ENTIRE SHOP WITHIN EASY REACH, CIRCUIT-RATED FOR SUFFICIENT AMPERAGE

STOCK FIRST AID KIT WITH MATERIALS TO TREAT CUTS, GASHES, SPLINTERS, FOREIGN OBJECTS AND CHEMICALS IN EYES, AND BURNS

HAVE TELEPHONE IN SHOP TO CALL FOR HELP

INSTALL FIRE EXTINGUISHER RATED FOR A-, B-, AND C-CLASS FIRES

WEAR EYE PROTECTION AT ALL TIMES

LOCK CABINETS AND POWER TOOLS TO PROTECT CHILDREN AND INEXPERIENCED VISITORS

USE DUST COLLECTOR TO KEEP SHOP DUST AT A MINIMUM

WEAR SHIRT SLEEVES ABOVE ELBOWS

WEAR CLOSE-FITTING CLOTHES

WEAR LONG PANTS

REMOVE WATCHES, RINGS, OR JEWELRY

KEEP TABLE AND FENCE SURFACES WAXED AND RUST-FREE

WEAR THICK-SOLED SHOES, PREFERABLY WITH STEEL TOES

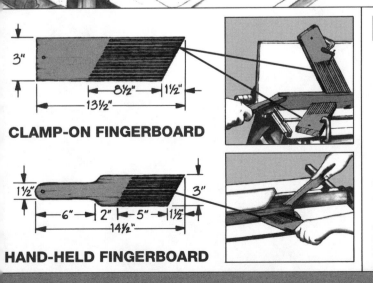

CLAMP-ON FINGERBOARD

3"
8½"
1½"
13½"

HAND-HELD FINGERBOARD

1½"
6"
2"
5"
1½"
14½"
3"

PROTECTION

WEAR FULL FACE SHIELD DURING LATHE TURNING, ROUTING, AND OTHER OPERATIONS THAT MAY THROW CHIPS

WEAR DUST MASK DURING SANDING AND SAWING

WEAR VAPOR MASK DURING FINISHING

WEAR SAFETY GLASSES OR GOGGLES AT ALL TIMES

WEAR RUBBER GLOVES FOR HANDLING DANGEROUS CHEMICALS

WEAR EAR PROTECTORS DURING ROUTING, PLANING, AND LONG, CONTINUOUS POWER TOOL OPERATION

THE WORKSHOP COMPANION™

MAKING BUILT-IN CABINETS

TECHNIQUES FOR BETTER WOODWORKING

by Nick Engler

Rodale Press
Emmaus, Pennsylvania

If you have any questions or comments concerning this book, please write:
  Rodale Press
  Book Readers' Service
  33 East Minor Street
  Emmaus, PA 18098

About the Author: Nick Engler is an experienced wood-worker, writer, and teacher. He worked as a luthier for many years, making traditional American musical instruments before he founded *Hands On!* magazine. Today, he is a contributing editor to *Workbench* magazine and has written over 30 books on the wood arts. He teaches woodworking at the University of Cincinnati.

Series Editor: Jeff Day
Editors: Roger Yepsen
        Bob Moran
Copy Editor: Sarah Dunn
Graphic Designer: Linda Watts
Graphic Artists: Mary Jane Favorite
                Chris Walendzak
Photographer: Karen Callahan
Cover Photographer: Mitch Mandel
Proofreader: Hue Park
Indexer: Beverly Bremer
Typesetting by Computer Typography, Huber Heights, Ohio
Interior and endpaper illustrations by Mary Jane Favorite
Produced by Bookworks, Inc., West Milton, Ohio

Library of Congress Cataloging-in-Publication Data

Engler, Nick.
    Making built-in cabinets/by Nick Engler.
        p.   cm. — (The workshop companion)
    Includes index.
    ISBN 0–87596–139–8 hardcover
    1. Built-in furniture. 2. Cabinetwork. I. Title
    II. Series:
    Engler, Nick. Workshop companion.
    TT197.5.B8E54 1992
    684.1'6—dc20   92–14079
                                            CIP

    6 8 10 9 7   hardcover

Special Thanks to:

Robertson's Cabinets
West Milton, Ohio

Wertz Hardware
West Milton, Ohio

CONTENTS

TECHNIQUES

1. **Cabinet Design**   2
   Standard Shapes and Sizes   3
      Standard Cabinet Dimensions   10
   Designing Your Own Cabinets   12
      Designing Kitchen Cabinets   19

2. **Cabinet Construction**   22
   A Construction Overview   23
   Unit Construction   27
      Fitting Allowance   35
      Buying Plywood and Particleboard   37

3. **Making Cabinet Cases**   39
   Working with Sheet Materials   40
   Case Joinery   44
      Plywood Cutting Aids   45
   Case Assembly   59
      Adjustable Router Guide   61
      Pocket Hole Jig   64
      Flush Trim Router Base   68

4. **Doors, Drawers, and Shelves**   69
   Making and Hanging Doors   70
   Making and Installing Drawers   75
   Installing Adjustable Shelves   78

5. **Installing Cabinets and Countertops**   **80**

    Installing Cabinet Units   81

    Installing Countertops   85

       Support Blocks and Deadmen   *88*

       Working with Laminates   *91*

PROJECT

6. **Putting It All Together: A Cabinetry Project**   **98**

Index   **122**

TECHNIQUES

1

CABINET DESIGN

The word "cabinet" comes from the French *cabinette,* meaning a small, one-room cottage. The term was first used in a woodworking context in the early seventeenth century. During that time, the upper class in Europe displayed their fine dinnerware or "plate" as a mark of their social status, and craftsmen devised elegant cupboards with glazed doors for just that purpose. Some of these china cupboards were so large and elaborate that one anonymous French wag compared them to the cabinettes of the peasants that dotted the countryside. The name stuck, and the craftsmen who made these impressive pieces began to call themselves "cabinetmakers."

Since that time, the term has evolved to mean many things. "Cabinet" no longer refers to a specific piece of furniture, but a broad range of pieces. Cabinets, to most people, are storage systems for various areas in their homes — kitchen cabinets, bathroom vanities, linen cupboards, entertainment centers, and bookshelves, to name a few. Instead of holding just dinnerware, cabinets now store almost everything.

Furthermore, most people think of *built-in* storage when they hear the word "cabinet." Modern built-in cabinets have three characteristics in common:

■ First, they're attached to the wall, floor, or ceiling and once installed, they become a fixed part of the architecture. Many cabinets rely on this connection for much of their structural strength.

■ Second, they're usually made from *sheet materials* such as plywood or particleboard. As the earliest cabinetmakers discovered, to make a large piece of furniture from solid wood, you must carefully plan the joinery to let the broad panels expand and contract. Because sheet materials are much more stable than wood, the construction can be much simpler.

■ Finally, large systems are made up of smaller *modules.* Each module is a box that holds drawers or shelves, and is fitted to the adjoining modules. This simplifies both construction and installation.

STANDARD SHAPES AND SIZES

BUILDING BLOCKS

Think of the cabinet modules as building blocks, sized and arranged to fit the available space. You can use as many or as few of these blocks as you wish when designing a cabinet system. The largest, most complex cabinets you can imagine can be broken down into small, easy-to-build boxes. Furthermore, there are just three basic types of boxes to build (*See Figure 1-1*):

■ *Counter units* rest on the floor and are usually about waist-high. The top provides a table or work surface, and the case can be filled with drawers, shelves, or a combination of both.

■ *Wall units* hang on the wall, normally at eye level, and may extend up to the ceiling. The cases are typically filled with shelves. (It would be difficult to see and reach the interior of drawers that hang at eye level or above.)

■ *Tall units* rest on the floor and extend above the waist, often to the ceiling. The lower portions can be filled with shelves and drawers; the higher parts normally hold shelves only.

There are two basic configurations for each box — one lies flat against a wall, the other turns a corner. Most cabinet units are built with a *rectangular* cross section to lie flat against a wall. However, you can build a unit with a *pentagonal* cross section to fit neatly in a corner. (*See Figure 1-2.*) You also can make a cabinet system turn an inside corner by butting two rectangular units together, but the storage space that's tucked back into the corner will be difficult to reach. Pentagonal or *corner* units make this space more accessible. (*See Figure 1-3.*) They are slightly more difficult to build, but not overly so.

Look over the cabinets in *Figures 1-4 through 1-6*. All of these storage systems look distinctly different and are used for diverse purposes. However, they all have been built the same way, from various combinations of the same three basic modules — base units, wall units, and tall units. Most of these modules are standard rectangular units, while a few are configured to fit in corners.

WALL UNIT

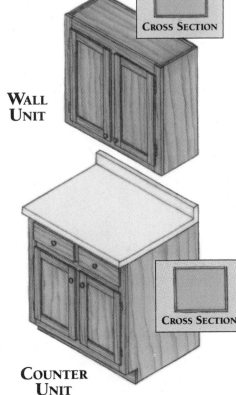

1-1 No matter how elaborate a cabinet system may seem, it's made up of just three simple modules. A *counter unit* provides a work surface as well as storage (drawers and shelves) beneath the counter. A *wall unit* offers storage space (shelves only) at eye level. When you don't need a work surface, a *tall unit* affords the maximum amount of storage space (drawers and shelves) for the floor space it occupies. Normally, each of these units is built as a large box with a *rectangular* cross section. This makes the unit relatively easy to build. It also makes the modules in the system easy to fit together.

COUNTER UNIT

TALL UNIT

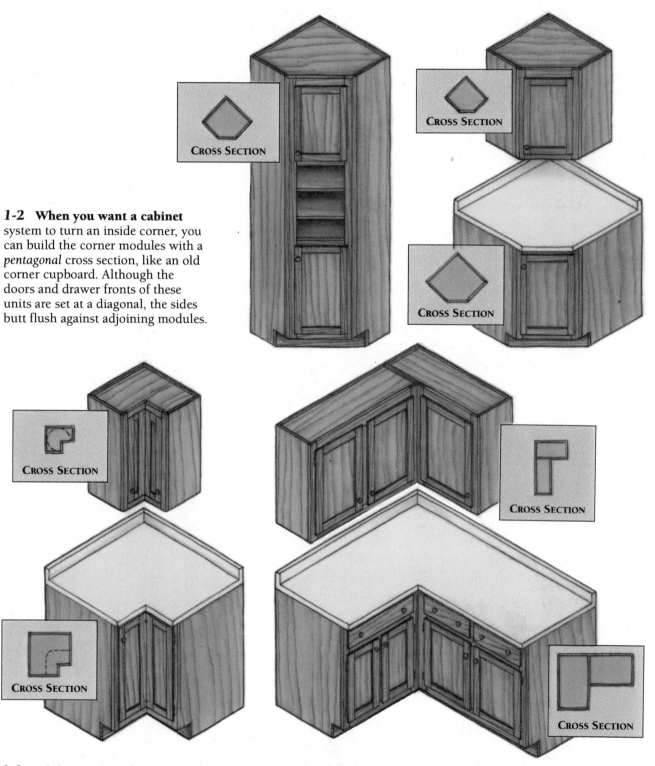

1-2 When you want a cabinet system to turn an inside corner, you can build the corner modules with a *pentagonal* cross section, like an old corner cupboard. Although the doors and drawer fronts of these units are set at a diagonal, the sides butt flush against adjoining modules.

1-3 While corner units are a useful way to make a cabinet system turn an inside corner, they are not the only choice. You can simply butt two rectangular cabinets against one another. Unfortunately, this makes the storage space in the corner hard to reach. Corner units, although more difficult to build than rectangular units, allow you to reach directly into the corner space. You can also use an L-shaped module, a hybrid between corner and rectangular units. These are often equipped with carousels or other special hardware to make the interior space more accessible.

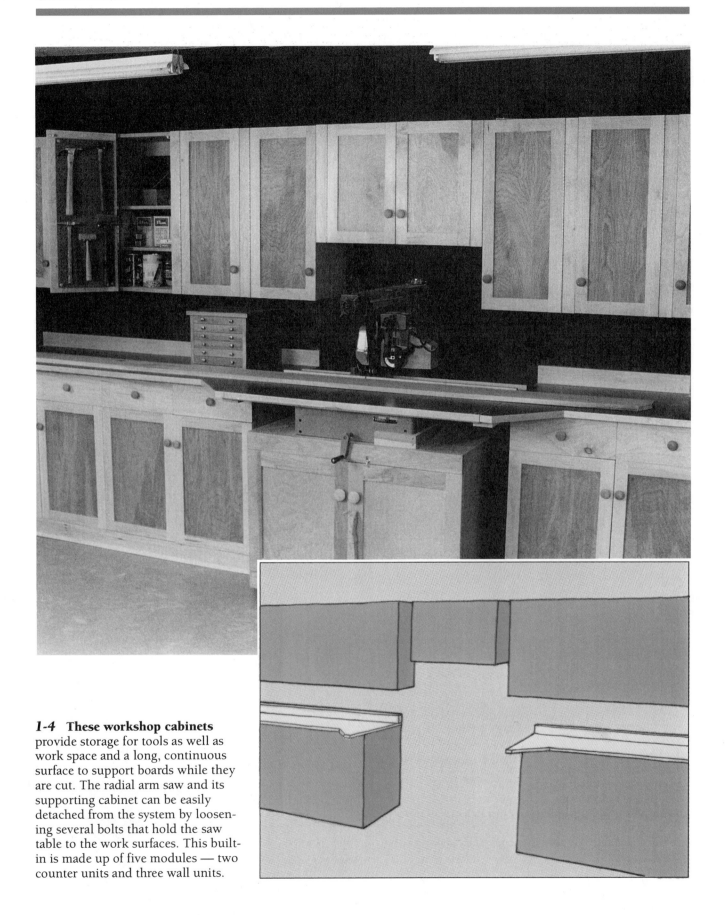

1-4 These workshop cabinets provide storage for tools as well as work space and a long, continuous surface to support boards while they are cut. The radial arm saw and its supporting cabinet can be easily detached from the system by loosening several bolts that hold the saw table to the work surfaces. This built-in is made up of five modules — two counter units and three wall units.

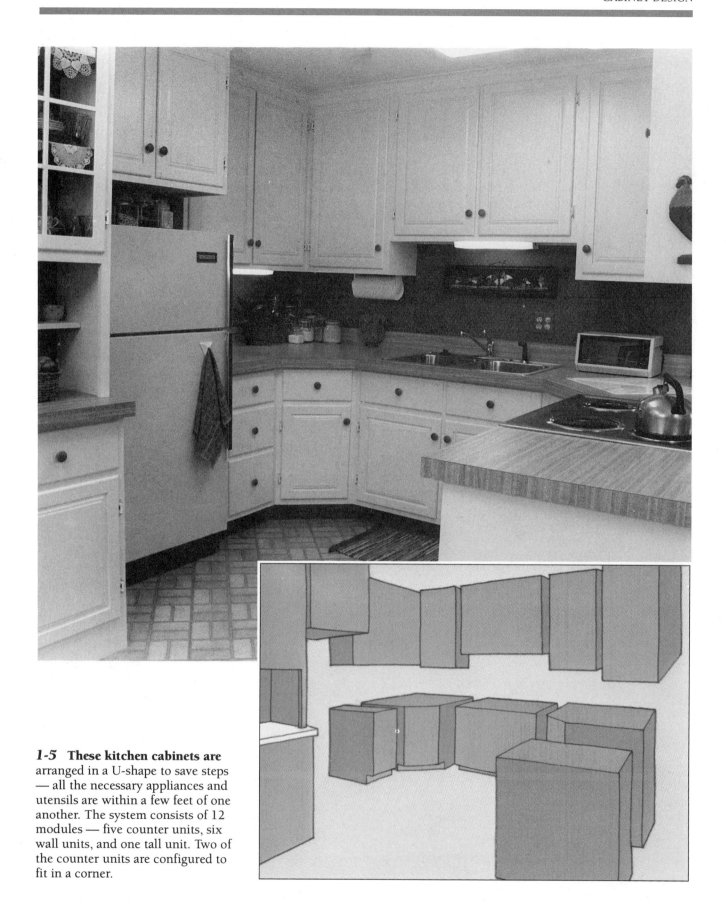

1-5 These kitchen cabinets are arranged in a U-shape to save steps — all the necessary appliances and utensils are within a few feet of one another. The system consists of 12 modules — five counter units, six wall units, and one tall unit. Two of the counter units are configured to fit in a corner.

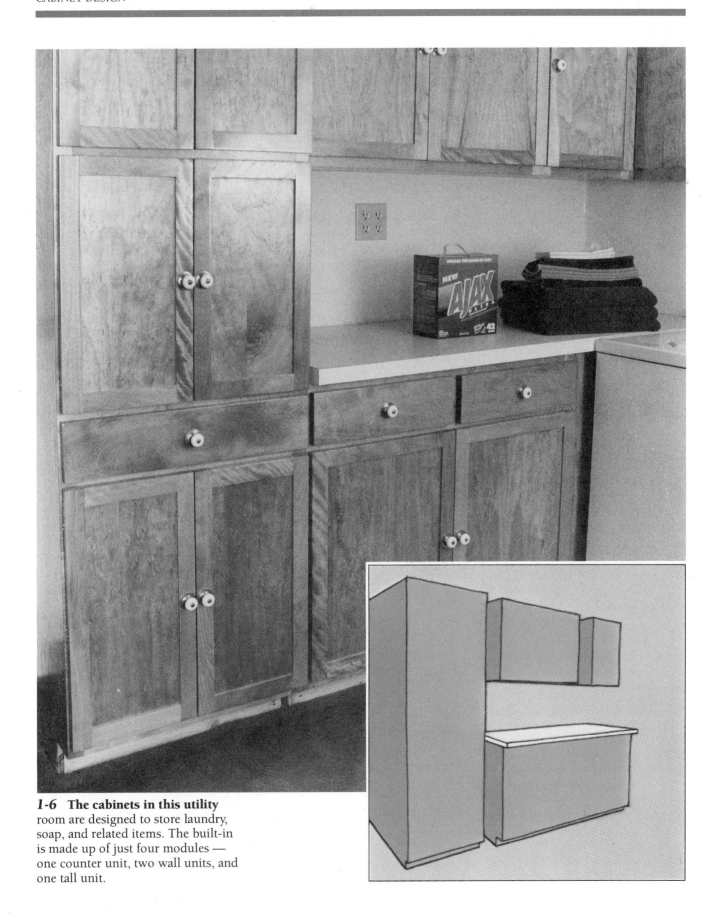

1-6 The cabinets in this utility
room are designed to store laundry,
soap, and related items. The built-in
is made up of just four modules —
one counter unit, two wall units, and
one tall unit.

STANDARD CABINET SIZES

There are no set sizes for these building blocks; you can alter them as needed to fit the available space. You can build each unit as deep (front to back), as wide (side to side), or as high (top to bottom) as you see fit. This is, perhaps, the biggest advantage to making your own cabinet units instead of purchasing them ready-made. You can work to your own specifications, rather than making do with someone else's measurements.

However, many cabinetmakers appreciate guidelines, if for no other reason than to have a point of departure. These are the accepted standard cabinet dimensions in North America:

■ *Counter units* are 24 to 25 inches deep and 36 inches tall. Kitchen and bathroom counters, which need to be durable, are often 1¼ to 1½ inches thick; elsewhere, counters are usually ¾ to 1 inch thick. Kitchen and bathroom counters overhang the cases by 1½ to 2 inches, making the depth of the work surface 25½ to 27 inches; elsewhere, counters may overhang by as little as ¾ inch. Kitchen and bathroom cabinets often have a toe space, normally 3 inches deep and 4 inches high. There is no standard for the width of counter units, but they are rarely less than 12 inches wide. Owing to the standard sizes of sheet materials, they are rarely more than 96 inches wide.

■ *Wall units* vary more than counter units. The standard depth is 12 inches, although it's not unusual to find them anywhere from 8 to 15 inches deep. They are normally 30 to 42 inches tall, but are frequently built shorter or taller. Like the counter unit, the width can be any measurement from 12 to 96 inches. If a wall unit is mounted above a counter unit, the space between the two should be 16 to 18 inches.

■ *Tall units* are often built as a combination of counter and wall units. The depth varies between 12 and 25 inches. The height is usually 60 to 84 inches, but they can be as high as the ceiling. And like the counter and wall units, the width can be anywhere from 12 to 96 inches. Tall units are often built in two parts, top and bottom, to make them easier to build. This split normally occurs at counter level, 36 inches above the floor. The top portion is sometimes shallower than the bottom, giving the unit the profile of an old-time hutch. (*SEE FIGURE 1-7.*)

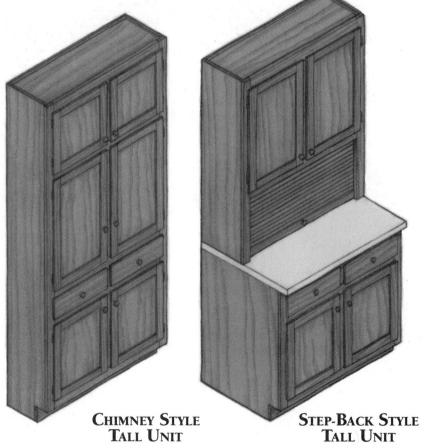

1-7 You can build a tall unit in either of two styles, depending on your tastes and needs. The straight or *chimney* style is a constant depth from top to bottom. In the step-back or *hutch* style, the top portion is narrower than the bottom. The step normally occurs at counter level, 36 inches above the floor.

**CHIMNEY STYLE
TALL UNIT**

**STEP-BACK STYLE
TALL UNIT**

■ *Corner units* are normally sized to fit adjoining modules. The sides are often the same depth and height as the units that butt against them. The standard width of *corner wall units* is 23 to 24 inches; the diagonal depth (the distance from the back corner to the front) is about 25 inches. The width of *corner counter units* is between 36 and 38 inches; the diagonal depth is approximately 43 to 45 inches.

FOR YOUR INFORMATION

Ready-made cabinets come in standard widths, usually starting at 12 inches wide and then increasing in 3-inch increments to 60 or 72 inches, depending on the manufacturer. Sometimes you can save time and money when making a large cabinet system by purchasing several ready-made modules, then building nonstandard units to match.

In addition to standard cabinet sizes, there are also standards for the sizes of doors, drawers, and shelves:

■ *Doors* of counter units are normally about 26 inches tall to allow room for a toe space or apron at the bottom and a drawer at the top. Doors of wall units can be as tall as the unit itself. The width of doors varies greatly, but a good rule of thumb is to keep them 18 inches wide or less. You don't want them to open too far out into the room where they would interfere with traffic.

■ *Drawers* vary between 5 and 10 inches tall. The top drawer is usually 5 to 6 inches tall, and successively lower drawers become taller by 1-inch increments. For example, if the top drawer is 5 inches tall, the next drawer down is 6 inches tall, then 7 inches, and so on. The bottom drawer can be taller than this 1-inch custom dictates, if that's what's needed to take up the extra space. (**Note:** There are rarely more than four drawers stacked up in a counter unit.) Like doors, drawer widths vary greatly, but if drawers and a door are positioned directly over or under each other, they usually have the same width.

■ *Shelves* are normally as deep as the inside of the cabinet case. However, in counter units and 24-inch-deep tall units, it's sometimes useful to make *half-shelves,* just 10 to 12 inches deep. (*SEE FIGURE 1-8.*) The shelves can be as wide as the cabinet, but if they are much wider than 36 inches, they may sag in the middle. For this reason, long units often require dividers. The spaces between fixed shelves vary from 8 to 16 inches, typically. Shelves built to hold specific items, such as canned goods or audio-video components, can be spaced accordingly. Or, you can install adjustable shelves. For a pictorial reference of standard dimensions, see "Standard Cabinet Dimensions" on page 10.

1-8 Unlike full shelves, half-
shelves do not span the full depth of
the cabinet case. This lets you store
tall items in front of the shelf and
short items above and below it.

STANDARD CABINET DIMENSIONS

Counter Unit
A. Depth . . . . 24″ to 25″
B. Height . . . . 36″
C. Width . . . . .12″ to 96″
D. Countertop thickness in kitchens
    and bathrooms . . . . 1¼″ to 1½″
    Elsewhere . . . . ¾″
E. Countertop overhang in kitchens and
    bathrooms . . . . 1½″ to 2″
    Elsewhere . . . . ¾″ to 2″
F. Backsplash height . . . . .4″ to 12″
G. Toespace depth . . . . .3″
H. Toespace height . . . . .4″

Wall Unit
I. Depth in kitchens . . . . .12″ to 13″
    Elsewhere . . . . .8″ to 15″
J. Height in kitchens . . . . .30″ to 42″
    Elsewhere . . . . Varies
K. Width . . . . .12″ to 96″
L. Height above counter . . . . .16″ to 18″

Tall Unit
M. Depth . . . . .12″ to 25″
N. Height . . . . .60″ to 84″
    (or to ceiling)
O. Width . . . . .12″ to 96″
P. Step-back or two-part design:
    Step or split occurs 36″ above floor

Corner Counter Unit
Q. Diagonal depth . . . . .43″ to 45″
R. Width . . . . 26″ to 38″

Corner Wall Unit
S. Diagonal depth . . . . .25″
T. Width . . . . 23″ to 24″

Doors
U. Height on base units . . . . .26″
    Elsewhere . . . . Varies
V. Width . . . . No more than 18″

Drawers
W. Height of top drawer . . . . 5″ to 6″
    Lower drawers become taller by 1″ increments
    up to 10″
X. Width . . . . Varies
    (often matches door above or below)

Shelves
Y. Depth of shelves . . . . To fit unit
Z. Depth of half-shelves in counter unit . . . 10″ to 12″
AA. Width . . . . Up to 36″
BB. Spacing . . . . .8″ to 16″

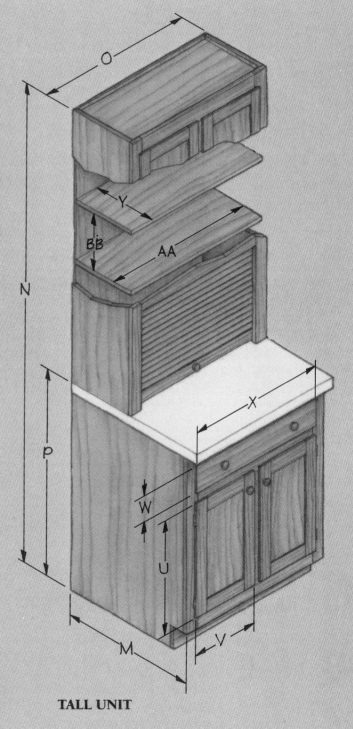

TALL UNIT

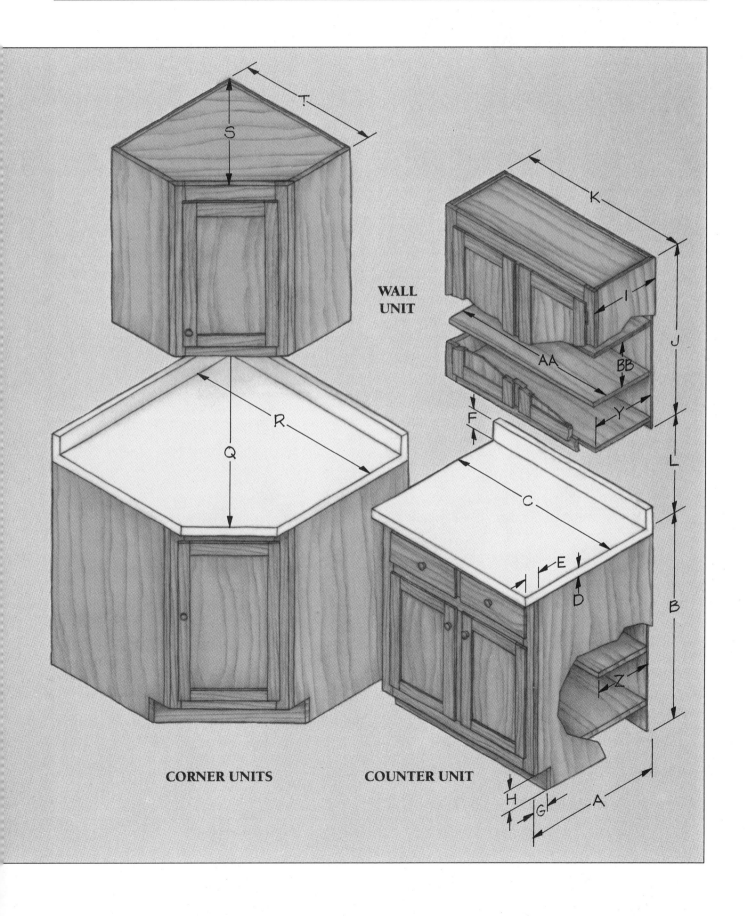

WALL UNIT

CORNER UNITS

COUNTER UNIT

DESIGNING YOUR OWN CABINETS

CHOOSING A STYLE

What cabinet style appeals to you? How do you want the completed system to look? All cabinet styles can be grouped into two broad categories:

■ *Traditional* cabinets (sometimes called American-style cabinets) have a face frame — a lattice of wooden strips that frames the openings for the doors and drawers. These strips also hide the front edges of the plywood or particleboard case parts. *(SEE FIGURE 1-9.)*

■ *Contemporary* cabinets (also called European-style cabinets) have no face frame. Instead, the front edges of the sheet materials are hidden by wooden strips, veneer, or plastic laminate. *(SEE FIGURE 1-10.)* Without face frames, contemporary cabinets present fewer horizontal and vertical lines to the eye. For this reason, they look simpler or "cleaner" than traditional cabinets.

Within each of these categories, there are many possible variations. You can use different species of wood, plywood veneers, or plastic laminates for a wide range of colors and textures. Or apply paints, stains, or bleaches to the wood or veneer to alter the color further. Make and mount the doors and drawers in various ways, or use different types and styles of hinges, pulls, and other hardware. Attach moldings and trim to create different visual effects.

How do you choose among all these possibilities? The best method is to study books and magazines of decorating ideas and select the design elements that appeal to you — wood species, colors, doors, drawer fronts, hardware, moldings, and trim. As you consider each of these elements, ask yourself these questions:

■ Will the texture, color, and style work well with your other home furnishings? For example, do you really want to build a contemporary-style entertain-

1-9 *Traditional* **cabinets have a** face frame that covers the front edges of the case parts. Although the doors and drawers can be installed in a variety of ways, usually each door and drawer front is rabbeted all around the circumference. This creates a lip which laps over the face frame members, while the rabbeted portion fits inside the frame opening. The knuckles of the door hinges are normally exposed.

1-10 *Contemporary* **cabinets** dispense with the face frame. Instead, the front edges are faced with thin materials. Like traditional cabinets, doors and drawers can be mounted many different ways, but most often they overlay the front edges of the case. The door hinges are usually completely hidden.

ment center in your den when most of your furniture is traditional country or Early American?

■ Will this style be easy to clean and maintain? Moldings, trim, and ornamental hardware are all dust catchers. Part of the appeal of the contemporary style is that the broad, flat surfaces are easier to wipe clean. This can be an important feature, particularly in a kitchen, bathroom, or child's room. On the other hand, nicks and scratches are more noticeable on broad surfaces.

■ Do you have the time and equipment to build cabinets in this style? Although most cabinet systems use the same basic construction, details often require special effort. A frame-and-panel door, for example, requires more time to build than one made from a single sheet of plywood. And if you want to shape the edges of the door frame, do you have a tool to do the shaping?

■ How much will this style cost? Some cabinet design elements cost much more than others. For example, a solid maple butcherblock countertop may run two to four times the cost of a laminate-covered counter. Your choice of hardware can also significantly affect cost — some hidden hinges for contemporary cabinets are twice the cost of traditional offset hinges.

■ How will this style affect the value and salability of your home? Built-ins — particularly kitchen and bathroom cabinets — can increase the selling price of your home and make it significantly easier to sell.

MAKING MEASUREMENTS

While you are considering the style you want, take some careful measurements — not just of the room where you will build the cabinet system, but of everything that will remain in the room *after* you install the system. This includes:

■ Locations of windows, doors, and other architectural features

■ Locations of plumbing and wiring, including pipes, taps, light switches, and outlets

■ Furniture that will remain in the room

■ Items you plan to store in the completed cabinets

■ Appliances, plumbing, or electronic components you plan to install in the cabinets

■ Special hardware you plan to install in the cabinets, such as carousels and slide-out shelves

■ You and anyone else who must use the cabinets

When making measurements of the room, windows, doors, and utilities, some professionals prefer to make several *story sticks* — long rulers made of one-by-three stock. It's best to create a vertical and a horizontal stick for *each wall* of the room. (*See Figure 1-11.*)

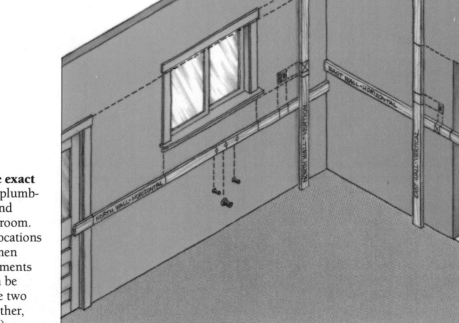

1-11 Story sticks show the exact locations of windows, doors, plumbing pipes, electrical outlets, and other important features in a room. They also show the planned locations of the cabinets. (Some craftsmen mark the two sets of measurements in different colors so they can be easily distinguished. Since the two are superimposed on one another, costly mistakes are less likely.)

These sticks show the exact locations of all the relevant features *and* the planned locations of the cabinets. This information is useful not only in the planning stage, but also while you're building and installing the cabinets. Additionally, story sticks save a lot of running back and forth. They give you a full-size reference that you can keep in your shop.

You may also wish to make horizontal and vertical *scribe strips,* particularly if you will install the cabinets in an older home. (*SEE FIGURE 1-12.*) As a house settles, frequently the walls bow or buckle slightly. A scribe strip shows the curvature of the walls. This, in turn, tells you how much extra stock to use when building the cabinet units so you can fit them to the wall.

TRY THIS TRICK

Use the same slender board for both your story sticks and scribe strips. Mark the room and cabinet measurements on one face of each one-by-three board, then turn the board over and scribe the curvature of the wall.

If you plan to install new appliances, such as a stove or a sink, in the cabinet system, purchase these *before* you start construction so you can measure them precisely. Do *not* trust the measurements on advertising flyers. At the very least, go to the appliance store and measure the items you intend to purchase.

The same applies for special hardware you want to install in the cabinets — brackets; baskets; sliding towel holders; carousels; lazy Susans; platform swivels; swing-out, slide-out, swing-up, or pop-up shelves; fold-up or fold-down ironing boards; or any of the contraptions sold to enhance storage space. (*SEE FIGURE 1-13.*) Not only do you need the precise measurements of each piece of hardware, you need to see *how they mount* in the cabinets.

The last item on the measuring list — you and the other people who will use the cabinets — is the most frequently overlooked; yet, in many ways, it's the most important. To get the maximum use out of your cabinets, they should be comfortable for you. If you're short, you may not want to run for a step stool every time you need to reach something on a high shelf. If you're tall, you don't want to constantly bump your head on low cabinets. Adjust the dimensions and the positions of the units in your cabinet system to accommodate your own physical attributes and preferences. (*SEE FIGURE 1-14.*)

1-12 To make a scribe strip, hold a long, straight scrap of wood against the wall. (You may need a helper to do this.) Measure the largest gap between the board and the wall, and adjust a compass to this measurement. Hold the point of the compass against the wall and the pencil over the board, then pull the compass along the wall. As the point traces the wall's curvature, the pencil transfers it to the board.

1-13 A quick browse through any
hardware catalog shows that there
are many mechanical marvels that
will enhance the storage space in
your cabinets. Here are just a few
(clockwise from top left): Swing-out,
half-round shelves allow you to
access corner storage space without
building corner cabinets; a special
basket mounts inside a cabinet door
to organize the lids of pots, pans,
and plastic containers; a pull-out
wastebasket slides in and out of a
counter cabinet; and fold-out trays
mount in the front of a sink unit to
store soap, scrubbers, and sponges.

1-14 When making custom
cabinets, you don't have to adhere
religiously to standard sizes. Make
the cabinets easier and more comfortable to use by adjusting the height
and depth of the work surfaces and
shelves to fit your own special needs.
This drawing shows the comfortable
reach and work surface levels for
two individuals, one 5 feet 8 inches
tall, and the other 6 feet 2 inches.

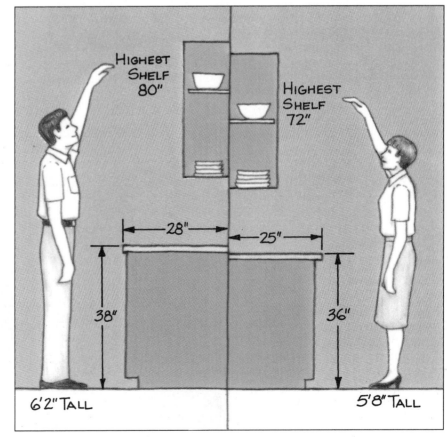

DRAWING UP A PLAN

When you have chosen a style and made the necessary measurements, draw up a plan to work from. It's important that these drawings be done to scale to give you an accurate idea of how the cabinets will fit and what they will look like. This requires no special drafting skills or training, just a little patience and basic arithmetic. Most office supply and drafting stores offer special architect's rules and graph paper to help you make scale drawings without a lot of figuring.

If you're installing a large system (such as kitchen cabinets), begin by making a two-dimensional sketch of the cabinets as viewed from the top. Divide the cabinets up into easily built units. This drawing will show you how many units you must build, how they will join together, and how the cabinets will fit in the room. You may wish to make several sketches, showing possible cabinet layouts and combinations of units, then pick the one that seems to work best. (SEE FIGURE 1-15.)

Once you have an acceptable top view, sketch a front view. If the cabinets will be attached to more than one wall, make a front view for each wall. Draw the division between the units, then fill in the doors, drawer fronts, and any open shelves. This will give you a good feel for how the cabinets will look after you install them and how much storage space they will offer. (SEE FIGURE 1-16.) If necessary, adjust your plans to get the look you want and the storage space you need.

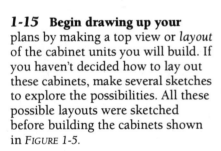

1-15 Begin drawing up your plans by making a top view or *layout* of the cabinet units you will build. If you haven't decided how to lay out these cabinets, make several sketches to explore the possibilities. All these possible layouts were sketched before building the cabinets shown in FIGURE 1-5.

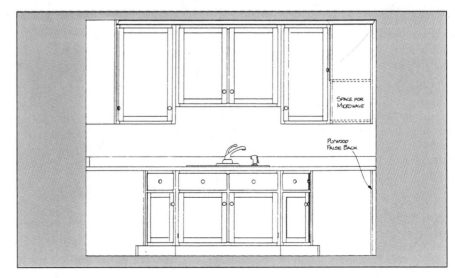

1-16 Of all the layouts shown in FIGURE 1-15, it was decided that the U-shaped floor plan worked best. A draftsman turned the layout into front views, or "elevations", of the three walls, showing how the installed cabinets would probably look. Compare this plan of the south wall, or the base of the U, with FIGURE 1-5.

WHERE TO FIND IT

If you don't trust your drawing skills, there is another planning aid available to help visualize your cabinetry project. You can buy a plastic grid with vinyl stick-on pictures of cabinet units shown from the top, side, and in three dimensions. These sets are available from many bookstores, or write:

Plan-A-Plex
Procreations Publishing Company
8129 Earhart Blvd.
New Orleans, LA 70118

Don't skip this step! It's impossible to underestimate the value of an overall plan when building a system with several components. If your cabinet system is particularly large or involved, you may want to hire an architect or draftsman to draw up the final plans. (This may be necessary if you live in an area where a major cabinetry project requires a building permit.) The money you pay a professional for accurate, detailed plans can save you many unpleasant and costly surprises further down the road.

ESTIMATING THE MATERIALS

Once you have a good set of plans and accurate measurements for each of the units in your cabinet system, make two lists — a cutting list and a list of materials. The cutting list shows the dimensions of each part of each unit — *every* part in the cabinet system you plan to build. The list of materials condenses the cutting list and totals up the duplicate parts. You can also use it to generate a shopping list of the raw materials you need to build the cabinets — sheets of plywood or particleboard, solid lumber, laminates, veneers, and hardware.

Make the cutting list first. Write down all the units in the cabinet system (east middle wall unit, southeast corner base unit, west tall unit) and the overall dimensions of each unit. Then, under the name of each unit, list all the parts in that unit, including shelves, doors, and drawer parts. Starting with the overall dimensions, figure the thickness, width, and length of the case parts (sides, back, dividers, fixed shelves, toeboards), then the face frame parts (if any), then the shelves, doors, and drawer parts. After each set of dimensions, write down the material you will use to make the part (plywood, particleboard, hardwood, softwood). (*SEE FIGURE 1-17.*)

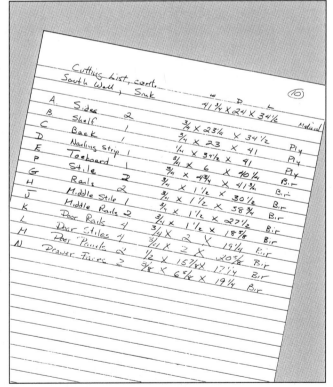

1-17 Before you can estimate the materials you need, you must make a *cutting list,* figuring the dimensions of each part in each unit in the cabinet system. This is a small portion of the cutting list from the kitchen cabinets shown in *FIGURES 1-5, 1-15, AND 1-16.*

Note: If you suspect a cutting list will take a long time to prepare, you're absolutely right. But this is a necessary step for all but the smallest cabinetry projects. It will save a great deal of work and possible confusion later on.

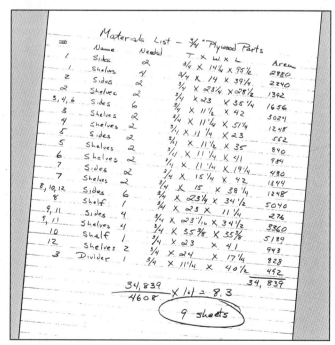

TRY THIS TRICK

When preparing the cutting list, use a pocket calculator that adds and subtracts fractions. This will save you the frustration of having to convert fractions into decimals and back again. There are many inexpensive calculators that will perform this function, available from any office supply or electronics store.

Use the cutting list to help prepare the list of materials. Make a list of the parts, organized by general type and material (case parts/plywood, case parts/hardwood, face frame members/hardwood, and so on). Go through your cutting list carefully and transfer each part and its dimensions to the appropriate section of the list of materials. If you find that parts from one unit are exactly the same size *and* material as parts from others, don't write them all down. Add them together and record the number of duplicate parts under the appropriate column. (SEE FIGURE 1-18.) Also add together the number of screws, hinges, pulls, and other hardware that you'll need.

Finally, use the list of materials to figure the amount of plywood and lumber you must purchase. (The types and amounts of hardware should already be totaled.) Do this by adding up the total *area* (in square inches) of the various materials required, then dividing these totals by the appropriate figures to find the number of 4-by-8 sheets and board feet needed.

Multiply the width, length, and number of each part to calculate the surface area. Add up the total areas of all parts of the same material *and* thickness, with two exceptions: Add together all the solid lumber parts that are under 1 inch thick, and add together all those between 1 and 2 inches thick.

This will give you a surface area total for each of several different thicknesses of plywood, particleboard, and/or lumber. Divide the totaled numbers for plywood or particleboard by 4,608 (the number of square inches in a 4- by 8-foot sheet). Multiply the result by 1.1 to add 10 percent for waste, test pieces, and mistakes. Then round *up* to the nearest whole number to find the number of sheets of that partic-

ular thickness that you need to purchase. Example: In the kitchen cabinet project referred to in FIGURES 1-15 THROUGH 1-18, the total area for ¼-inch plywood parts was 28,654 square inches. That total, divided by 4,608 and multiplied by 1.1, equals 6.84. Rounding up, you find the cabinetmaker needed seven sheets of ¼-inch plywood.

Note: Some craftsmen prefer to sketch how they will cut the parts from the material. This is a useful exercise before cutting. For estimating, however, the mathematical method is just as accurate and less time consuming.

Next, calculate the number of board feet of lumber the job will require. To find the amount of *four-quarters* stock you need, divide the total area of lumber under 1 inch thick by 144; for the amount of *eight-quarters* stock, divide the area of lumber between 1 and 2 inches thick by 72. Multiply the results by 1.1 to add extra stock for waste. Example: In the kitchen cabinet project, the total area of solid wood parts under 1 inch thick was 8,740 square inches. That area, divided by 144 and multiplied by 1.1, equals 66.76. Rounding off, you get 67 board feet of four-quarters lumber.

1-18 This is part of the list of materials from the same project. Note that there are many duplicate parts. For example, there are six counter unit sides, all precisely the same size and cut from the same material.

DESIGNING KITCHEN CABINETS

Kitchen cabinets are perhaps the most complex home storage systems that you can design. They are complex not because they're particularly large or difficult to build, but because they require many special considerations.

Work triangle — The prime consideration is the work triangle. Kitchen designers have found that there are three important work centers in every kitchen — for food storage, cooking, and cleanup. These roughly correspond with the locations of the refrigerator, stove, and sink. Draw imaginary lines between these three areas to find your *work triangle*. If the triangle is very large, you may be wasting time and energy walking between the work centers. If it's very small, the kitchen may be cramped. Designers generally try to keep the triangle perimeter between 13 and 22 feet.

Minor work centers — In addition to the three major work centers, there are several others. Although these are not included in the work triangle, their proper sizing and placement will help make your kitchen more efficient and comfortable.

■ Include a *mixing center* in your design between the sink and refrigerator. Ideally, this should provide between 3 and 5 linear feet of counter space. Since you'll probably be using both the mixer and the blender at this location, there should be an electrical outlet.

■ There should also be a *food preparation center* between the stove and the sink. There are a large number of appliances associated with food preparation (toasters, countertop ovens, electric griddles and fry pans, crockpots, popcorn poppers, and so on), so this center requires more counter space than a mixing center — 3½ to 6 linear feet. It, too, should have at least one electrical outlet.

■ It's also helpful to create a *serving center* between the stove and the dining area, a place to keep prepared food before transferring it to the table. This needn't be large; 2 linear feet of counter space is adequate.

Major appliances — It goes without saying that you must give careful thought to appliances and utilities when designing a kitchen. But don't just consider what appliances you have or will soon

purchase; think about the future and what appliances you may add later. Or, just as important, what appliances might prospective home buyers want to add?

■ A 30-inch space was once considered adequate for a *refrigerator*, but as more and more families buy side-by-side models, the standard is now 36 inches. Also, provide a 1-inch space between the back of the refrigerator and the wall for ventilation, and make sure there's an electrical outlet nearby. If the appliance has an icemaker, or if you want to add one later, you will want a plumber to run a ¼-inch cold-water line to the refrigerator location.

■ *Sinks* vary widely in the amount of space they require, depending on the number and configuration of the tubs. For this reason, you need to purchase and measure the sink *before* building the cabinets. You may also want to leave room under the sink cabinet for a garbage disposal or water purifier. If your design moves the sink from its original location, you'll need a plumber to run lines to the new spot.

■ *Stoves* are more standardized than either sinks or refrigerators; most require 30 inches of linear space. But there are two ways to install a stove — you can either *drop* it into a cabinet or *slide* it into position between cabinets. You may also want to use a separate rangetop and oven so you can mount the oven beside or over the range. The oven will require adequate ventilation, and in many locations, exhaust hoods are required above ranges. All of these possibilities affect how you will build the cabinet system. Finally, plan to have an electrician run a 220-volt line to a relocated stove, range, or oven.

■ More and more, *microwave ovens* are built into kitchen cabinets. Since there is no standard size for these appliances, purchase and measure the oven you want *before* building the cabinets. Leave at least 1-inch space between the cabinet surfaces and the oven sides, top, and back for ventilation. (Some ovens require more top space — follow the manufacturer's recommendations.) Also, plan to have an electrical line run to the oven location.

(continued) ▷

DESIGNING KITCHEN CABINETS — CONTINUED

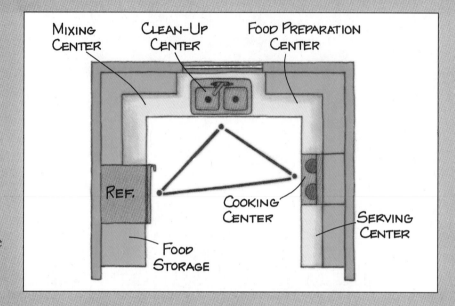

1 **Many architects and home** economists consider a U-shaped kitchen to make the most efficient use of space. The work triangle is clearly defined, and the work centers are close to one another.

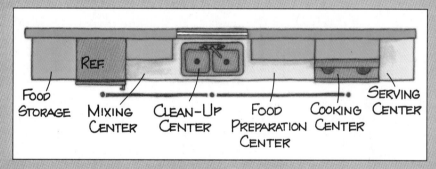

2 **By the same standards, a** strip kitchen is the least efficient. There is no real work triangle, and the work centers are widely separated.

3 **A galley kitchen, in which** the cabinets and major appliances occupy two walls on opposite sides of the room, is an efficient layout provided the two walls are close enough to one another.

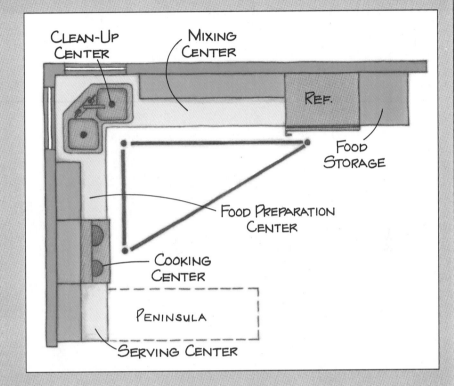

4 **In an L-shaped kitchen, the** cabinets and appliances occupy two adjoining walls. Although this is an improvement over a strip kitchen, it's not nearly as efficient as a U-shaped or galley kitchen. If you have the space, add a peninsula to one leg of the L.

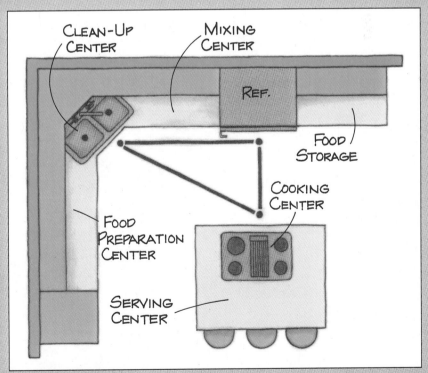

5 **You can also improve strip** and L-shaped kitchens by building an "island" out from the walls. This creates almost the same work triangle as a U-shaped or galley kitchen.

2

CABINET CONSTRUCTION

The construction of built-in cabinets seems light when compared to stand-alone furniture. The individual modules rarely require reinforcing bracework or sophisticated joinery. Cabinet units use as little material as possible and are usually assembled with elementary butts, rabbets, dadoes, and grooves. This extreme simplicity is possible because each unit derives much of its strength from the adjoining units and walls to which it's attached. The individual building blocks may look flimsy, but the completed structure is solid.

Cabinet construction is similar from module to module. Wall units, counter units, tall units, and corner units all use the same joinery and many of the same parts. This similarity is more than a convenience; it's almost a necessity to save time when building large cabinets. By using duplicate parts and joints, cabinetmakers can mass-produce large portions of a cabinet system.

A CONSTRUCTION OVERVIEW

Not only is cabinet construction similar from module to module, it's also similar from style to style. Although the cabinet systems in architectural design books and magazines may look very different, most are built in the same manner. They are distinguished instead by how they are decorated — the wood, veneer, laminate, stain, paint, moldings, trim, doors, and drawer fronts that are applied or attached to the boxes.

Cabinet construction is, in fact, fairly standardized — particularly case construction. If you look through other books on cabinetmaking, you may find minor differences from the basic designs shown here. In general, however, you'll see that all cabinets are built according to these simple rules of thumb (SEE FIGURE 2-1):

■ The sides of each cabinet module support most of the other parts of the case — back, face frame, toeboard, counter, fixed shelves, and so on. The only parts not supported directly by the sides are the vertical dividers, which must be mounted between horizontal parts.

■ The back of the cabinet serves to keep the unit square until it can be attached to a wall. It's attached to the back edges of the sides, dividers, and top and bottom shelves.

■ Each unit has one or more cleats or *nailing strips* at the back which are used to attach it to a wall. Some wall units have nailing strips at the top so they can be attached to the ceiling.

The most noticeable variation in cabinet construction is between traditional and contemporary styles. The cases of traditional cabinets have face frames; contemporary cabinets do not. (SEE FIGURE 2-2.) Surprisingly, the presence or absence of a face frame does not affect any other aspect of the case construction. With the exception of the frame, the cases for both styles are built almost exactly the same.

Note: You may wonder whether traditional cabinets, by virtue of their face frames, are stronger than contemporary cabinets. They are, but only to a small degree. Face frames do help to keep the cases square. But if the joints that hold the shelves and backs in place are well-made, contemporary cabinets can't be distorted easily. And once the units are all joined to each other and the supporting walls, a contemporary cabinet system will endure ordinary use and abuse just as well as a traditional one.

There are also differences in how the drawers and doors fit the cabinet case. An *inset* door or drawer front is flush with the front surfaces of the case; an *overlay* door or drawer front laps the case; and a *lipped* door or drawer front is somewhere in between the two. (SEE FIGURES 2-3 THROUGH 2-5.) Furthermore, there are several ways in which doors and drawers can be installed in the case. The type of doors and drawers you choose will affect the construction of these assemblies; the way in which you install them may affect the case construction to some degree.

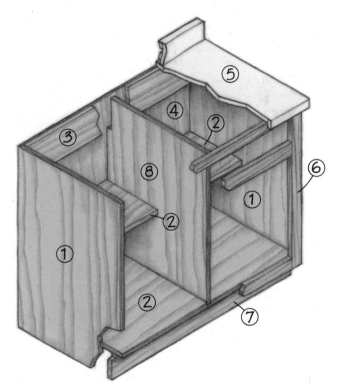

2-1 The *sides* (1) of a cabinet case support most of the other case parts and assemblies. The *fixed shelves* (2) — top shelf, bottom shelf, and middle shelves — rest in dadoes or rabbets in the sides. The *nailing strip* (3) is butted to the sides, and the *back* (4) fits into rabbets in the back edges of the sides. If the unit has a *counter* (5), it rests on the top edges of the sides. The *face frame* (6) — if there is one — butts against the front of the case; the *toeboard* (7) is recessed. Only the *dividers* (8), if used, are not directly attached to the sides.

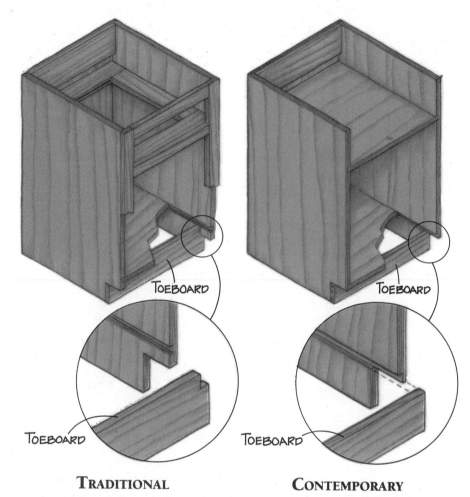

2-2 When making cabinet modules of different styles, you'll find the case construction is fairly standard — with one exception. On a traditional cabinet, you attach a face frame to the front edges of the cabinet sides; however, you omit the face frame on a contemporary cabinet. You may also want to adjust the position of the bottom shelf. On a traditional cabinet, the bottom shelf is usually installed slightly above the toespace. On a contemporary cabinet, the bottom shelf is even with the top of the toespace.

TOEBOARD

TOEBOARD

TOEBOARD

TOEBOARD

TRADITIONAL   **CONTEMPORARY**

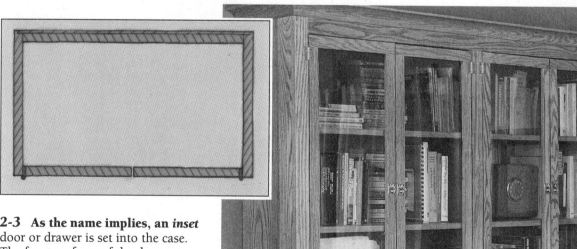

2-3 As the name implies, an *inset* door or drawer is set into the case. The front surfaces of the door are flush with those of the face frame, cabinet sides, and dividers. These are considered the hardest doors and drawers to install because they require more careful fitting than other types.

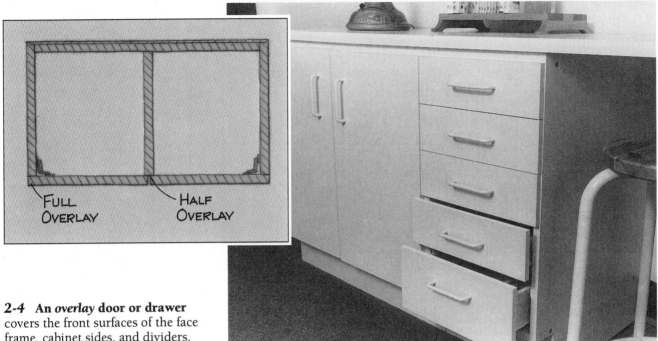

2-4 An *overlay* door or drawer covers the front surfaces of the face frame, cabinet sides, and dividers. If it is installed in a contemporary cabinet (without a face frame) and completely covers one edge of the case, it's considered a *full overlay*. If the door only covers the edge part- way, it's a *half overlay*. A single door or drawer front may fully overlay some edges and half overlay others, depending on how it's mounted. For example, cabinetmakers often install doors with full overlays at the sides and half overlays at the shelves and dividers.

2-5 The outside edges of a *lipped* door or drawer front are rabbeted. This rabbet forms a lip which covers the face frame or the front edges of the cabinet case. If an opening is covered by a single door or drawer front, the assembly is lipped on all four edges. If it's covered by two doors, and there's no mullion or divider to separate the doors, only three edges of each door are lipped. The adjoining edges are left square.

Finally, there is a difference in how doors and drawers are made. *Slab* doors are just single sheets of plywood or particleboard; *board-and-batten* doors are wooden boards held together with crossties; and *frame-and-panel* doors consist of a wide board mounted in a frame. (*SEE FIGURE 2-6.*) You can also omit the doors entirely, leaving the shelves open. (*SEE FIGURE 2-7.*) Drawers vary in how the parts are joined, but these

variations are less visible than the variations in doors. Door and drawer construction and installation are covered in more detail in "Doors, Drawers, and Shelves" beginning on page 69.

All these differences are superficial, however. The fact remains: Most cabinet construction is well standardized.

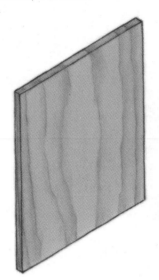

2-6 There are many ways to construct a door. Here are three of the most common: You can make a *slab door* from a single piece of plywood or particleboard. Or, you can join several solid boards with crossties or battens to make a *board-and-batten door*. Finally, you can build a frame around a wide board for a *frame-and-panel door*.

SLAB DOOR   **BOARD & BATTEN DOOR**   **FRAME & PANEL DOOR**

2-7 The shelving space in a cabinet does not have to be covered by doors. You can omit some or all of the doors, depending on the style of the cabinet and what it will be used for. These tall cabinet units have *open shelves* at the top and enclosed shelves or *cupboards* at the bottom.

UNIT CONSTRUCTION

While the construction of the basic cabinet modules is similar, it isn't precisely the same. Wall units, counter units, tall units, and their respective corner variations use many of the same parts and types of joinery, but each is assembled in a different way. There are, in fact, more differences between the construction of the basic modules than there are between different styles.

MAKING WALL UNITS

Wall units are the simplest of the basic modules. These are little more than boxes with a few shelves and dividers. (*SEE FIGURE 2-8.*)

Some units have nailing strips at the back so they can be attached directly to the wall. Other wall units — particularly those that are mounted over peninsulas or islands — have nailing strips at the top so they can be attached to the ceiling. Also, some cabi-netmakers prefer to use two-part mounting strips with interlocking edges rather than single nailing strips. (*SEE FIGURE 2-9.*) **Note:** Two-part mounting strips must be attached to the outside surface of the back (rather than the inside, like nailing strips). This complicates the construction, so cabinets with two-part mounting strips often have no back. Because backless cabinets are less sturdy, and because the interlocking edges of the mounting strips may split if the cabinets and their contents are too heavy, cabinets with two-part mounting strips are usually lightweight.

The construction of wall units is also affected by how the shelves are installed. *Fixed* shelves are set permanently in dadoes. *Adjustable* shelves, which can be raised or lowered, rest on movable pins or some other hardware which must be installed inside the cabinet. (*SEE FIGURE 2-10.*)

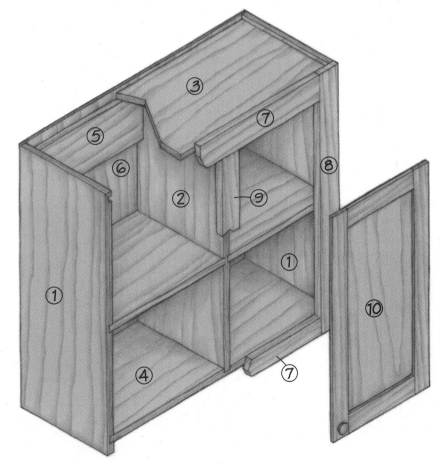

2-8 A typical wall unit is a simple box. There are two *sides* (1) and, if the unit is wide enough, one or more *dividers* (2). The sides are rabbeted or dadoed to hold the *top shelf* (3) and *bottom shelf* (4), and these shelves are dadoed to hold the dividers. The *nailing strip* (5) is nailed or screwed to the sides and top shelf, and the *back* (6) fits in rabbets in the sides, overlapping the nailing strip, top shelf, bottom shelf, and dividers. The face frame consists of *rails* (7) and vertical *stiles* (8), which cover the front edges of the sides and the top and bottom shelves. If there are any dividers, the face frame will also have one or more inside stiles or *mullions* (9) to cover them. The *doors* (10) hang on the stiles and mullions, or, in the absence of a face frame, on the sides and dividers.

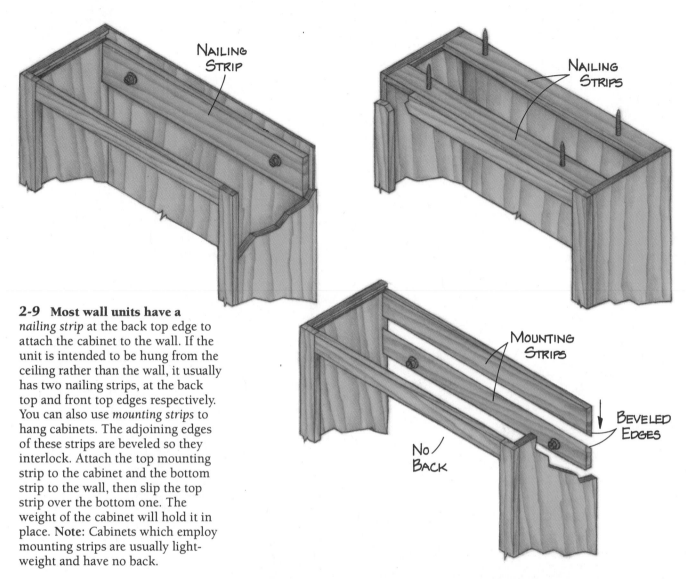

2-9 Most wall units have a *nailing strip* at the back top edge to attach the cabinet to the wall. If the unit is intended to be hung from the ceiling rather than the wall, it usually has two nailing strips, at the back top and front top edges respectively. You can also use *mounting strips* to hang cabinets. The adjoining edges of these strips are beveled so they interlock. Attach the top mounting strip to the cabinet and the bottom strip to the wall, then slip the top strip over the bottom one. The weight of the cabinet will hold it in place. **Note:** Cabinets which employ mounting strips are usually light-weight and have no back.

2-10 *Fixed shelves* are attached permanently to the sides and usually rest in dadoes. *Adjustable shelves* rest on pins or other movable hardware, and can be raised, lowered, or removed completely. On many cabinets, only the top and bottom shelves are fixed. All the middle shelves are adjustable.

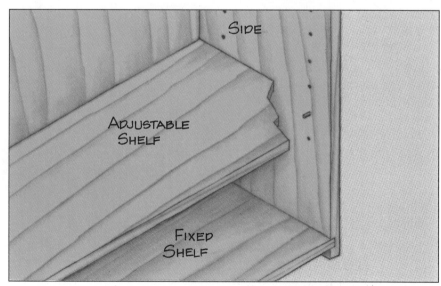

MAKING COUNTER UNITS

Counter units are more complex than wall units. First, they must have a solid base on which to rest, and this base frequently includes a toespace. Second, they support a work surface or counter. And finally, the interior is frequently filled with drawers as well as shelves. (SEE FIGURE 2-11.)

Fixed shelves and adjustable shelves each require slightly different construction, just as they do in the wall units. So do drawers, depending on whether they slide in and out of the case on wooden supports, brackets, side-mounted metal slides, or bottom-mounted slides. (SEE FIGURE 2-12.) Also, the addition of a toespace will slightly alter the way in which the units are built. (SEE FIGURE 2-13.)

Another significant variable is whether the counter unit will be attached to a wall or used as a freestanding peninsula or island. If freestanding, the construction must be more substantial than an attached counter unit. Additionally, the back and the back corners must be finished to appear as attractive as the front. (SEE FIGURE 2-14.)

TRY THIS TRICK

You can make an island or peninsula by butting two shallow, standard base units back to back, then covering them with a single wide countertop. This requires a little more material, but you don't have to build a special unit.

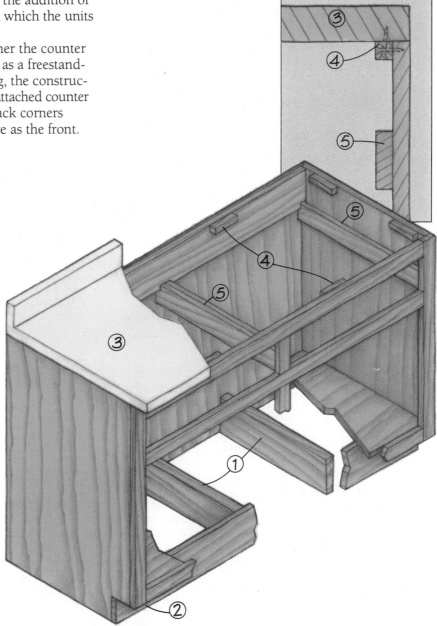

2-11 A typical counter unit is built in the same manner as a wall unit, but with some important additions. Since the cabinet will rest on the floor, the bottom shelf is often reinforced with *bottom supports* (1) — thick boards spaced every 16 to 24 inches to help support the weight. If the counter will be used as a work surface, the base is recessed to make a *toespace* (2). The *counter* (3) rests on the top edges of the sides, nailing strip, and face frame, and is held in place with screws and *cleats* (4). If there are drawers in the cabinet, you must also add some form of *drawer support* (5).

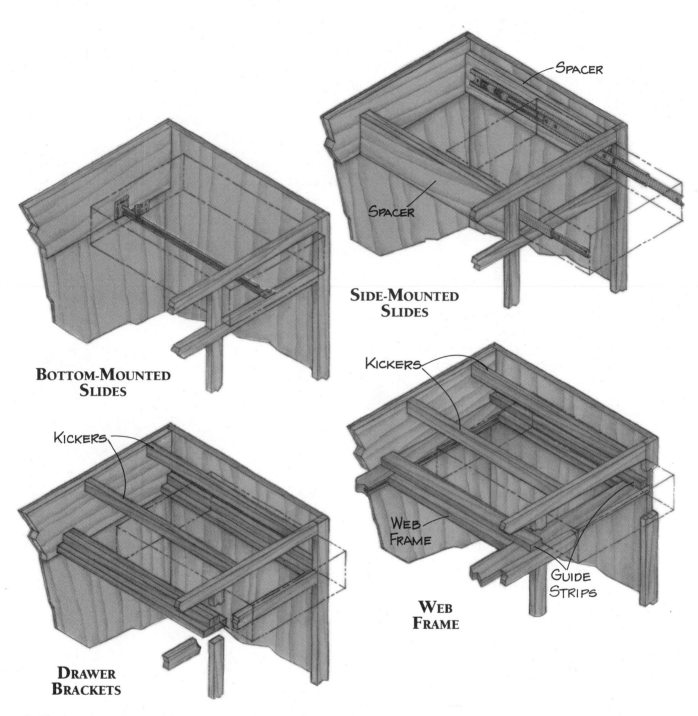

SIDE-MOUNTED SLIDES — SPACER, SPACER

BOTTOM-MOUNTED SLIDES

WEB FRAME — KICKERS, WEB FRAME, GUIDE STRIPS

DRAWER BRACKETS — KICKERS

2-12 There are four common ways to install a drawer in a cabinet, and each requires that the case be built in a certain way. Perhaps the easiest way is to use *bottom-mounted slides* (available in both metal and wood). These attach to the face frame and the nailing strip, and require no additional wood parts. Metal *side-mounted slides* are more stable and

support more weight than bottom-mounted slides, but they sometimes require attaching wooden spacers or mounting blocks to the cabinet sides and dividers. If you need to save money on hardware or would rather make an all-wood system, you can attach wooden L-shaped *drawer brackets* to the face frame and nailing strip to support and guide the

drawer. Or you can use a traditional *web frame* with guide strips. This requires more work and materials than drawer brackets, but it's more durable and supports more weight. Both drawer brackets and web frames may require *kickers* — strips of wood mounted above the drawers to keep them from tipping when pulled out of the cabinet.

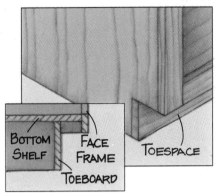
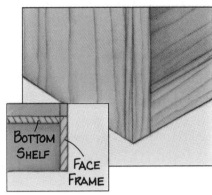

2-13 A toespace is faced with a *toeboard,* which is attached to the front edges of the sides and bottom supports. If there is no toespace, the face frame extends to the floor and the bottom rail serves as a toeboard.

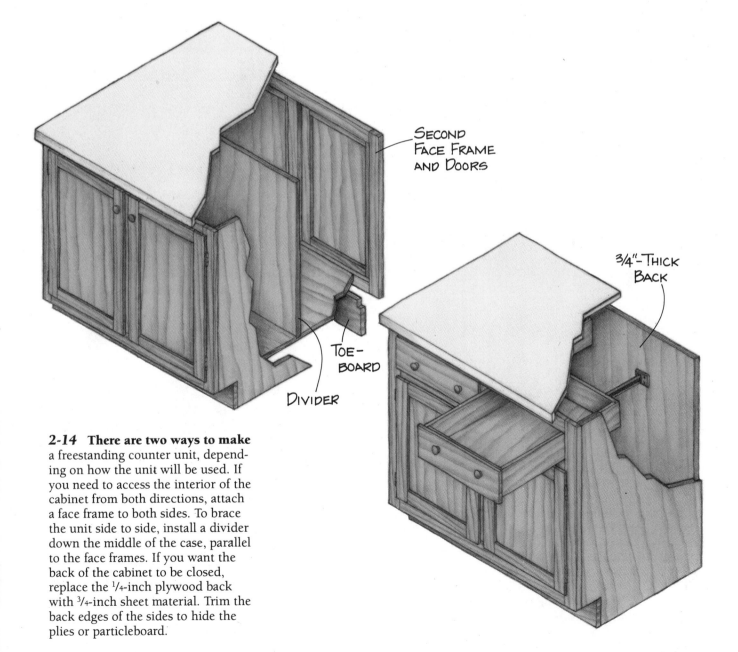

SECOND FACE FRAME AND DOORS

DIVIDER

TOE-BOARD

3/4"-THICK BACK

2-14 There are two ways to make a freestanding counter unit, depending on how the unit will be used. If you need to access the interior of the cabinet from both directions, attach a face frame to both sides. To brace the unit side to side, install a divider down the middle of the case, parallel to the face frames. If you want the back of the cabinet to be closed, replace the 1/4-inch plywood back with 3/4-inch sheet material. Trim the back edges of the sides to hide the plies or particleboard.

MAKING TALL UNITS

Tall unit construction, as you might expect, combines most of the features and variables of wall and counter units — toeboards, drawers, fixed and adjustable shelves. (*See Figure 2-15.*) You also have to decide whether to make the unit in one piece or two. Because tall units become so large, cabinetmakers sometimes design them as two parts — upper and lower. (*See Figure 2-16.*) This makes them easier to build and install.

Tall units are often built to hold appliances or electronics. In a kitchen, they will often house a microwave or eye-level oven. In living rooms and dens, they become entertainment centers and audio/video cabinets. This, too, affects construction. The interior space must be ventilated to prevent heat build-up, and you may have to provide pathways for wires and cables. (*See Figure 2-17.*)

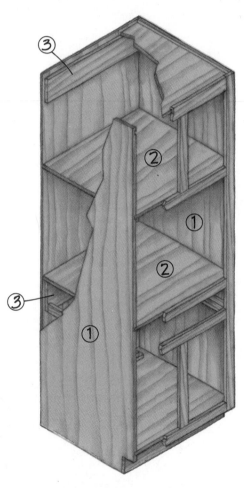

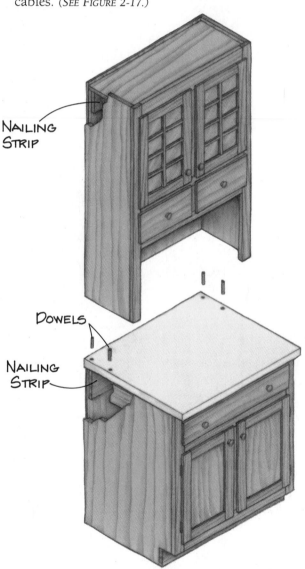

2-15 A tall unit is constructed like an extended base unit — the *sides* (1) can stretch from floor to ceiling. In addition to the top and bottom shelves, there are usually one or two fixed *middle shelves* (2) attached to the side. Sometimes a middle shelf *is* a countertop, with open space above it for room to work. And there are typically two *nailing strips* (3) — one at the top of the cabinet, and one just below a middle shelf.

2-16 Oftentimes, it's easier to build large tall units in two parts — upper and lower, with the division at the middle (countertop level) shelf. When installing them, fasten the two parts together with screws or dowels. Then attach each part to the wall using the nailing strips.

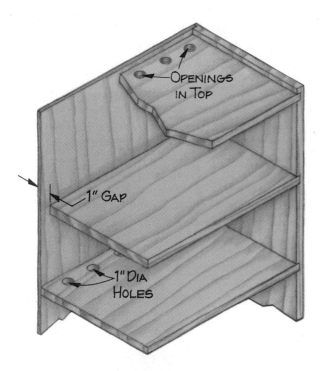

2-17 To ventilate a cabinet for
appliances or electronic components,
drill several 1-inch-diameter holes
near the back edge of each shelf. You
also can leave a 1-inch gap between
each shelf and the back of the
cabinet. Both of these methods allow
the hot air to rise, preventing heat
from building up inside the cabinet.
They also make it easier to run wires
and cables between the shelves.

MAKING CORNER UNITS

You can adapt each of the basic units so it turns a corner. As mentioned previously, a corner unit has a *pentagonal* cross section, rather than the simple rectangle
of standard units.

The construction of a corner unit is similar to that
of a standard module, with these exceptions (*SEE
FIGURE 2-18*):

■ Corner units have five sides — a front, two sides,
and *two* backs (left and right) joined at right angles.
This allows the unit to fit in a corner.

■ The left and right backs serve the same structural
purposes as the sides; that is, they help support the
shelves and other horizontal case parts. Like the sides,
they are often cut with dadoes and rabbets in which
the top, bottom, and middle shelves rest. For this
reason, they must be thicker than a standard back.

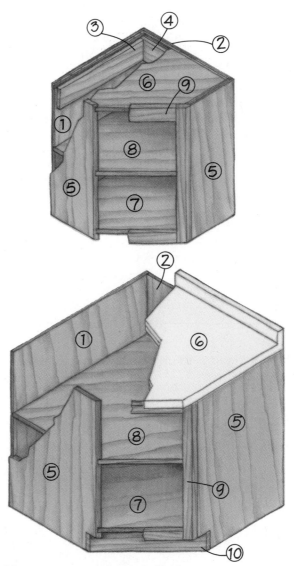

2-18 A corner unit has two backs
— a *left back* (1) and a *right back*
(2). These are made from ½- or ¾-
inch plywood or particleboard, and
are joined at right angles to one
another. The unit may also have two
nailing strips — a *left nailing strip*
(3) and a *right nailing strip* (4).
These, too, are joined at right angles.
The backs fit in rabbets in the *sides*
(5). Both the backs and the sides are
dadoed or rabbeted to hold the five-
sided *top shelf* (6), *bottom shelf* (7),
and any *middle shelves* (8). The front
edges of the sides are beveled and
the *face frame* (9) is attached at a
45 degree angle to each side. The
toeboard (10) is also attached at a 45
degree angle to the sides.

The backs of corner units are normally ½ inch thick, although some cabinetmakers prefer to make the backs of counter units and tall units from ¾-inch-thick stock.

■ Some cabinetmakers dispense with the nailing strip, especially on corner counter units and corner tall units, since the back is thick enough to be attached directly to the wall.

■ The face frame (if there is one) joins the front edges of the sides at 45 degree angles. When the cabinet is installed in a corner, the face frame will be 45 degrees from each wall.

FOR BEST RESULTS

Do not make the backs of corner wall units thicker than ½ inch. You want these units to be as light as possible since they hang from the walls.

There aren't as many variables in the construction of corner units as there are in other modules. They usually have fixed shelves set in dadoes; it's difficult (sometimes impossible) to get adjustable five-sided shelves in and out of corner cases. Frequently, they are fitted with round, revolving shelves — carousels, lazy susans, or turntables. (*SEE FIGURE 2-19.*) None of this hardware requires special construction. It all screws or bolts in between two fixed shelves.

You can install drawers in a corner unit, although it's not often done because so much potential storage space is wasted. Drawers affect the construction of corner cabinets the same way they do in standard units. You must add the proper supports to the cabinet interior to mount the drawer guides or slides. (*SEE FIGURE 2-20.*)

2-19 Carousels and other revolving shelving units help to make the interior space of a corner unit more accessible. They're fairly easy to install — drop them in the cabinet before attaching the counter-top and bolt them in place. (You can also drop them in from the *side* — just leave one cabinet side unattached until you do so.) Although the cabinets must be properly sized, you rarely need to modify the construction to accommodate this hardware.

2-20 Perhaps the easiest way to add a drawer to a corner unit is to use a fixed shelf as a drawer support. To guide the drawer, attach wooden strips to the shelf at right angles to the face frame or front opening. Not only is this construction simple, the fixed shelf also provides a solid mount for hardware should you want to install revolving shelves under the drawer.

FITTING ALLOWANCE

All too often, there will be gaps between cabinets and walls. Although plywood and particleboard sheets may seem perfectly flat, they rarely are, and slightly bowed or warped stock will make cabinets that aren't precisely square. And even if square cabinet units, they may not fit together perfectly if the room isn't square or the walls aren't flat. There are two ways to deal with these problems. You can cover up unsightly gaps with moldings and trim. Or, if you want to avoid the gaps altogether, you can build each unit with a *fitting allowance* — extra stock on the sides and at the back that can be scribed and cut for a perfect fit.

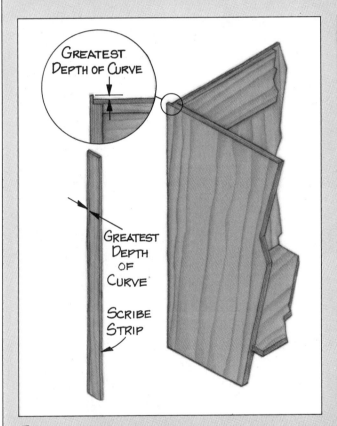

1 **To create a fitting allowance** at the back of a cabinet unit, cut the rabbets that hold the back slightly deeper than the thickness of the back. How much deeper? Refer to your *vertical* scribe strip (see page 14) and measure the greatest distance between the curved line on the strip and the edge of the strip that was held against the wall. If this distance is ¼ inch, and the back is ¼ inch thick, cut the rabbets ½ inch deep (the sum of the two).

2 **When installing the cabinet** units, slide each one against the wall where it will be attached. Scribe the curve of the wall on the side of the cabinet, using a compass as you did to trace the curve on the scribe strip. Cut this curve with a saber saw or coping saw. **Note:** Scribing and cutting the back edges of a cabinet requires much time and patience. For this reason, many cabinetmakers prefer not to mess with this particular fitting allowance unless the wall is badly bowed.

(continued) ▷

FITTING ALLOWANCE — CONTINUED

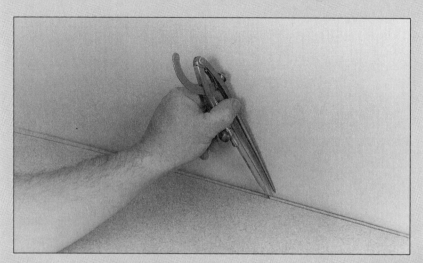

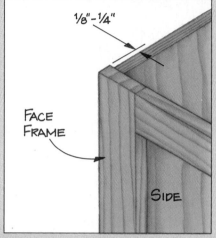

3 **For counter units, you may** also want to cut the countertop slightly wider than the plans specify. Refer to the *horizontal* scribe strip (see page 14) to determine just how much wider. When installing the cabinets, butt the back edge of the counter up against the wall, scribe the curve of the wall on the counter, then cut the curve.

4 **When making traditional** cabinets, you can create a fitting allowance at the sides to compensate for warped sides or bowed walls. Make the face frame slightly wider than the plans call for so it protrudes past the cabinet sides. The side allowance is much harder to estimate than the back allowance since it depends on the size and shape of the cabinet unit as well as the unevenness of the parts and wall. But the rule of thumb is to leave ⅛ to ¼ inch extra stock on the sides.

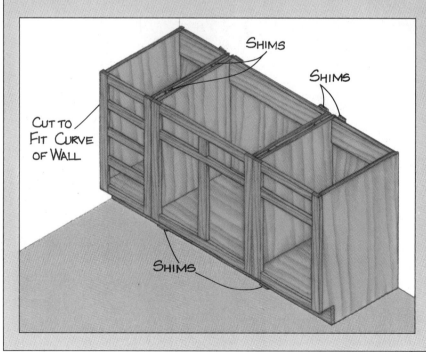

5 **When installing the cabinet** units, fasten them together so all the overhanging *face frames* are flush, with no gaps between them — even though there may be gaps between the cabinet sides. Additionally, the top edges of counter units must be straight and level with one another. If necessary, use wooden shims between the individual units or between the units and the wall or floor to keep the cabinets properly aligned. If the side of a unit butts up against a bowed wall, scribe the curvature of the wall on the face frame, then cut the curve with a saber saw or coping saw.

BUYING PLYWOOD AND PARTICLEBOARD

There are many types and grades of plywood and particleboard. Each type and grade has a specific purpose. To choose the right material for your cabinets, you must first understand what these types are and how they are graded.

Plywood — Two types of plywood are commonly used in cabinetmaking. Most cabinets are built from *hardwood plywood*, which can be made from many different species of hardwood and is extremely strong. *Softwood plywood* is normally used in construction, but the better grades are well-suited to cabinetry.

Plywood is graded with a two-character code, each character indicating the quality of one of the veneer faces. Each type is graded differently.

Hardwood plywood:

SP indicates a "specialty" grade. This plywood is made to order for a particular buyer. Often, the veneer is specially matched.

A is the "premium" grade. The veneer pieces are carefully joined, usually with matched grain.

1 indicates the "good" grade. The veneers are not matched, but the pieces do not contrast sharply.

2 is the "sound" grade. There are no open defects, but there may be small knots, discolorations, and sharp contrasts between veneers.

3 is the "utility" grade. It's similar to the sound grade, but the knots may be bigger and there may be some small splits.

4 indicates the "backing" grade. There may be open knotholes and large splits.

Softwood plywood:

N indicates a smooth veneer which will look good with a natural finish. The veneer pieces are all heartwood or all sapwood, carefully joined and matched. This grade is not commonly available; you may have to special-order it.

A is smooth with a few repairs. It looks okay with a natural finish, but there may be a noticeable contrast between the veneer pieces.

B has a solid surface with tight knots, repair plugs, and small splits.

C-Plugged has small, open knots and splits, but the larger defects are repaired. These repairs may be made with putty rather than wooden plugs.

C indicates medium-size open knots, splits, discoloration, and sanding defects, as long as these do not affect the strength of the panel.

D has large knots and other defects. Because these may impair the strength of the panel, the uses of this grade are limited.

What grades should you purchase? Generally, cabinetmakers choose A-2 (A on one side and 2 on the other) or better hardwood plywood for the outside (visible parts) of cabinets and 1-2 or 1-3 for the inside. When buying softwood plywood, look for N-B or A-B for the cabinet exterior, and no less than B-B for the interior.

There are other types of plywood you may consider for specific applications. If you can't hide the edges of the plywood parts, *lumber core plywood* is more attractive than hardwood and softwood plywood because it has fewer plies. It also holds screws and nails better. It's not as strong as other types, but its strength is adequate for most cabinetry projects. If you plan to paint your cabinets, consider *medium density overlay (MDO) plywood*. This has a thin, resin-impregnated paper overlay on one or both sides and provides a perfectly smooth base for paints.

Particleboard — "Particleboard" is a generic term for several different types of sheet materials made from ground-up bits of wood, glued together and pressed into sheets. The size of these bits varies from individual wood fibers (as in fiberboard) to large chips (as in waferboard). Most of the particleboard used in cabinetry is made from sawdust- and shaving-size particles.

Particleboard is graded with a three-character code. The first character indicates the application (inside or outside); the second, the density of the material; and the third, the size of the wood particle used to make the material.

(continued) ▷

BUYING PLYWOOD AND PARTICLEBOARD — CONTINUED

Application:

1 tells you that the particles are bonded together with a glue (usually urea-formaldehyde) intended for interior uses only.

2 indicates the glue (usually phenol-formaldehyde) will endure both the weather outdoors and wet locations.

Density:

H denotes high density. This material weighs over 53 pounds per cubic foot.

M indicates medium density. The material weighs between 38 and 53 pounds per cubic foot.

L means low density, less than 38 pounds per cubic foot.

Particle size:

1 indicates the material is made from extremely small particles, only slightly larger than wood fibers. The surface tends to be very smooth.

2 is for run-of-the-mill sawdust-size particles. The surface is flat, but not smooth to the touch.

3 indicates large particles such as planer shavings. These produce a fairly rough surface.

F stands for "flakes," wood bits that are somewhat larger than sawdust or shavings. The resulting surface is very rough but fairly even.

W tells you that the material is made from large chips or "wafers," and the surface is likely rough and uneven.

Note: *F*- and *W*-type particles are commonly available only in exterior grades of particleboard.

Most of the particleboard used in cabinetmaking is made with interior glue and has a medium density. The particle size depends on how the material will be used in the cabinet. Cabinetmakers generally make case parts from 1-M-1 and 1-M-2 particleboard, and countertops from 1-M-2 and 1-M-3. Shelving can be made from 1-M-1, 1-M-2, or 1-M-3. None of these interior grades are strong enough to use for cabinet backs, but 2-M-W particleboard works well for this application.

Most particleboard is made from sawdust-size bits of wood. Unless the particles are extremely small, the surface is not smooth to the touch. But it is flat and even.

Some particleboard, such as this "cedar closet lining," is made from planer-shavings-size bits, or *flakes*. The surface is much rougher and less even than ordinary particleboard.

Particleboard intended for structural use, such as roof sheathing or floor underlayment, is often made from chip-size pieces of wood or *wafers*. This is much rougher than particleboard made from sawdust or flakes, but it's also much stronger.

3

MAKING CABINET CASES

Once you have designed the cabinet system and have decided how to construct the various units, you can begin building. The best place to start is with the cabinet *cases* — the outside shell of each cabinet (excluding the countertop, if there is one) plus any dividers, fixed shelves, wooden drawer supports, nailing strips, or wooden hardware mounts included in the plans.

It's best to build *all* the cases at once before making any of the doors, drawers, or other subassemblies. First of all, this saves time. Because there are many duplicate parts and joints from unit to unit, it's easier to cut them all at once while the machinery is set up.

Second — and more importantly — you get a better set of cabinets. No matter how carefully you plan a cabinetry project, it always evolves as you build it. As you work, you can incorporate new ideas for better, more attractive ways to make this or that. If you build the system one unit at a time, you may not be able to take advantage of this inspiration — each cabinet must be the same as the first, or the installation could appear hodge-podge and poorly planned.

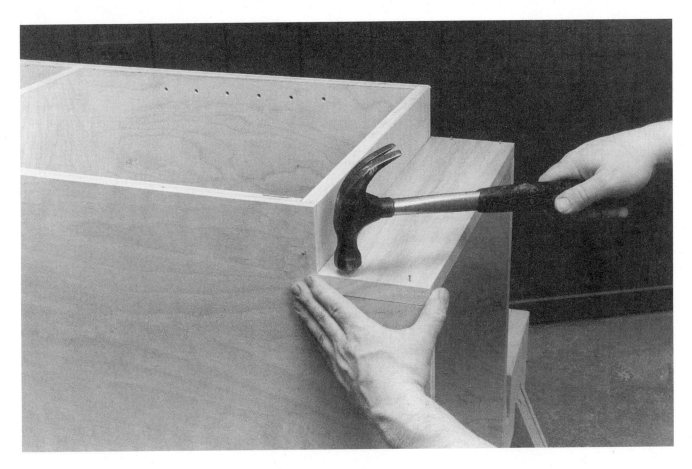

WORKING WITH SHEET MATERIALS

For many home craftsmen, the most daunting part of a cabinetry project is cutting up unwieldy 4- by 8-foot sheets of plywood and particleboard. Professional cabinetmakers have large panel saws to cope with this problem, but these tools require more space and more money than most of us can spare for occasional use. Fortunately, there is a way to cut sheet materials safely and accurately with ordinary home workshop tools and a few simple jigs.

HANDLING AND SUPPORT

Before making the first cut, you must be able to support an entire sheet at a comfortable working level. *This is extremely important!* You cannot make accurate cuts without properly supporting the workpieces. And you need more support than is afforded by ordinary sawhorses, which allow sheet materials to buckle as they're sawed. This pinches the blade and spoils the accuracy of the cut.

You need a *cutting table* — a surface large enough to hold a full sheet of plywood or particleboard and keep it flat *before and after* each cut. You can make your own cutting table by building a sturdy workbench with a 4-foot-wide, 8-foot-long top. This bench should be just 24 to 27 inches high, allowing you to lean over the sheet materials as you measure, mark, and cut them.

If you don't have room for a large workbench, make a simple grid of construction lumber supported by sawhorses. When assembled, the top edges of the grid members must be flush so the materials laid across them will remain flat. (*SEE FIGURE 3-1.*) You can

also use this setup as an assembly table by laying a sheet of plywood or particleboard across the grid to serve as a work surface. When you don't need the grid, take it apart and store the pieces.

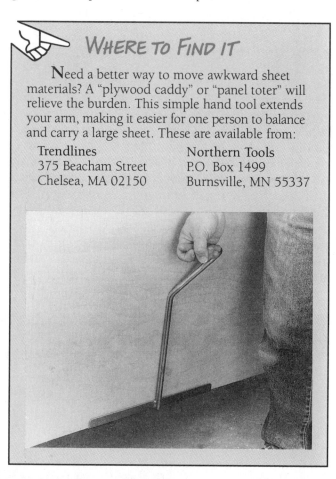

WHERE TO FIND IT

Need a better way to move awkward sheet materials? A "plywood caddy" or "panel toter" will relieve the burden. This simple hand tool extends your arm, making it easier for one person to balance and carry a large sheet. These are available from:

Trendlines
375 Beacham Street
Chelsea, MA 02150

Northern Tools
P.O. Box 1499
Burnsville, MN 55337

3-1 To support sheet materials at a comfortable level while you lay out and cut cabinet parts, build a *grid* of construction lumber. One of the simplest ways to make this grid is to build a pair of sawhorses, then tie them together with 2 x 4 beams running perpendicular to the horses. Although there's not much to it, this setup will support both large and small pieces of plywood and particleboard and keep them from sagging as you work. For plans and instructions on how to make this *Knockdown Plywood Cutting Grid,* see "Plywood Cutting Aids" on page 45.

LAYOUT AND CUTTING

With the plywood or particleboard properly supported, lay out the parts as accurately as possible. Use oversize layout tools: the larger and longer, the better. You can purchase extra-long framing squares and straightedges from most building supply centers and companies that handle drywall and masonry supplies.

TRY THIS TRICK

To lay out cuts on sheet materials easily, make an oversize T-square from two scraps of plywood. Remember, the arm must be attached to the base of the T at *precisely* 90 degrees. Check the accuracy of this homemade layout tool with a trustworthy framing square before using it.

As you mark the sheets, indicate the *waste* areas, or the *waste side* of the layout lines. This will help you to remember which side of the line to cut on.

When marking plywood, many craftsmen *score* the layout lines with a pocketknife or utility knife, cutting through the thin layer of veneer. This has two advantages. First, knives are more accurate marking tools than pencils. A knife always leaves a thin, consistent line; as a pencil point grows dull, however, the line broadens and it's difficult to know precisely where to cut. Second, because the knife cuts the veneer, it helps prevent chips and torn grain. (SEE FIGURE 3-2.)

There are two ways you can cut up the parts you've marked. The first is to cut them to size with a circular saw, using a long straightedge to guide the saw. Providing the straightedge is long enough to span the

entire cut, it will eliminate the inaccuracies of a hand-held saw. You can purchase 4-foot and 8-foot straightedges from many mail-order woodworking suppliers, or you can make your own. (SEE FIGURE 3-3.)

Most craftsmen, however, prefer to cut the parts in two steps. They first cut them slightly larger than needed with a circular saw, then trim the parts to the final sizes on a table saw. Although you must cut each part twice, this method eliminates the need to carefully position and clamp the straightedge to the plywood before each circular saw cut. Also, it's much easier to make accurate cuts on a table saw, using a fence or miter gauge to guide the work.

When using the two-step method, lay out the parts on the plywood or particleboard so each one has at least one *factory edge*. Although this edge may look a little ragged, it will be perfectly straight. Rough out the parts with a circular saw, then use the factory edge to guide the first table saw cut. After that, use either the factory edge or an edge that's been cut on the table saw to guide successive cuts. (SEE FIGURE 3-4.) Do *not* use edges that have been sawed with a circular saw as guides; these may not be perfectly straight.

3-2 When cutting plywood, *score* the layout lines with a knife to get a clean cut. The board on the left was laid out in pencil, and the saw blade has lifted and torn the plywood veneer where it exited the kerf. The board on the right was scored before it was sawed. Since the veneer was already severed, the blade did not lift it. The resulting cut is much cleaner.

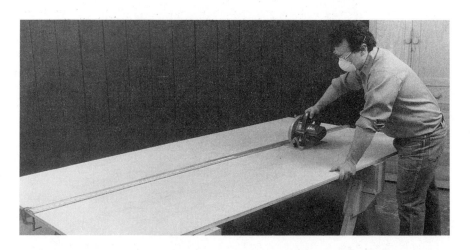

3-3 For accurate circular saw cuts, use a straightedge to guide the cut. You can purchase an 8-foot-long metal straightedge (shown) from most woodworking suppliers, or you can make your own. See the plans and instructions for the *Circular Saw Guide* in "Plywood Cutting Aids" on page 45.

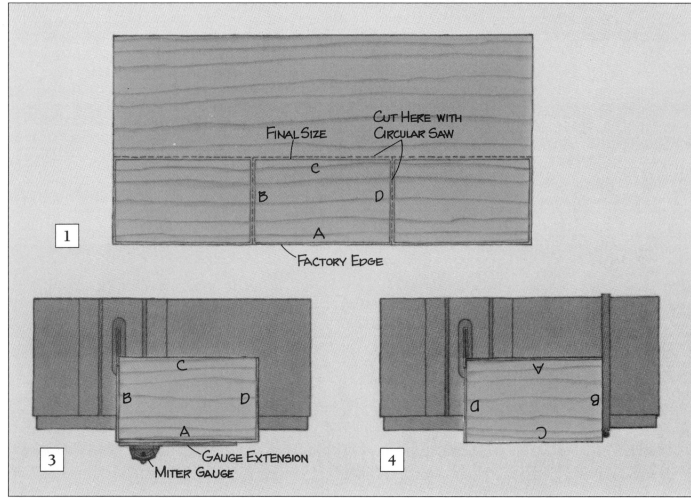

3-4 To cut a part from a large sheet of plywood or particleboard, rough it out with a circular saw, then cut it to its final dimensions on a table saw. (1) Lay out the part so it has at least one *factory edge* — A. With a circular saw, cut the part ¼ to ½ inch longer and wider than needed. (2) Using the rip fence as a guide, cut edge C, directly opposite the factory edge A. Don't cut the part to its final width yet; leave it just a little wide. (3) Next, trim edge B, using the miter gauge and extension to guide the cut. Again, don't cut the stock to its final dimension; leave it a little long. (4) Trim edge D, using either the rip fence or the miter gauge to guide the cut. This time, cut the stock to its final length. (5) Finally, trim the factory edge A,

When cutting large sheets of plywood on a table saw, ask someone to help you feed the stock. During the cut, make sure that either you or your helper can quickly reach the on/off switch, should you need to stop the saw. If the workpiece blocks the switch, use an auxiliary foot-operated switch.

What if there's no factory edge available, or the factory edge is too small to provide a sufficient guiding surface? Or, what if the piece is too long or too wide to cut using the table saw fence as a guide? In this case, you must use a *Trimming Guide* to cut the part. This simple shopmade jig lets you use any wooden straightedge to guide a cut. (SEE FIGURE 3-5.) It's also useful for duplicating parts or cutting odd-shaped parts that would otherwise require complex machine setups. (SEE FIGURE 3-6.)

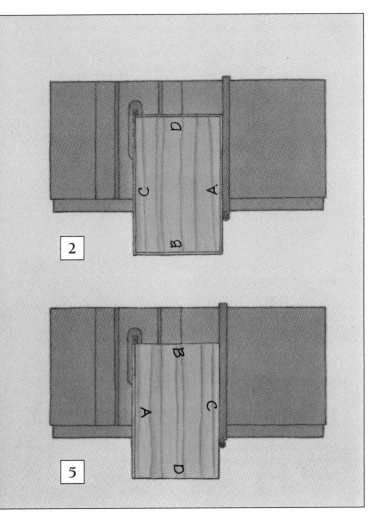

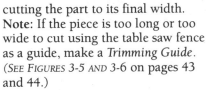

cutting the part to its final width. **Note:** If the piece is too long or too wide to cut using the table saw fence as a guide, make a *Trimming Guide*. (SEE FIGURES 3-5 AND 3-6 on pages 43 and 44.)

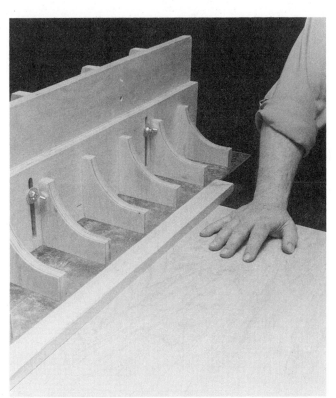

3-5 A trimming guide will help cut any plywood or particleboard edge perfectly straight, with no need to use a factory edge as a guide. This jig fastens to your table saw fence and extends over the saw blade. (For plans to make the *Trimming Guide* shown and for instructions on how to set it up, see "Plywood Cutting Aids" on page 45.) Line up a *wooden* straightedge with the layout line on the piece you want to cut. Fasten it in place with double-faced carpet tape. Feed the sheet material into the saw blade, letting the straightedge ride along the trimming guide. **Note:** You can make a wooden straightedge by jointing a long scrap.

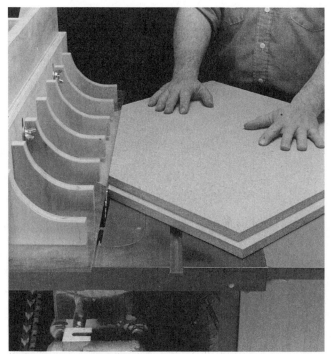

3-6 You can also use a trimming guide to duplicate parts precisely, as long as all the edges to be cut are straight. Make just one part, then rough out as many oversize blanks as you need. Fasten the part to a blank with double-faced carpet tape. Cut the blank to its final size and shape, using the part as a pattern and the trimming guide to guide the cuts. Repeat for the remaining blanks. This technique is particularly useful for duplicating the five-sided parts in corner cabinets.

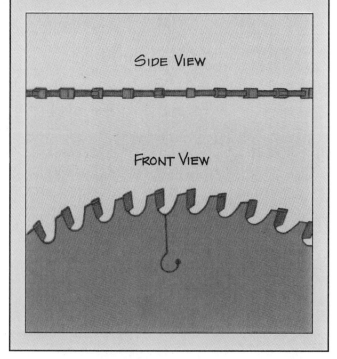

FOR BEST RESULTS

Whether you use a circular saw or a table saw to cut sheet materials, you should outfit the cutting tool with a blade that's suited for plywood and particleboard. The standard woodworking wisdom once was to use a special plywood blade for clean cuts in plywood and a combination blade for particleboard. However, there are now carbide-tipped blades with a *triple-chip grind* on the sawteeth that work well in both materials. These blades also make smooth cuts in solid wood.

SIDE VIEW

FRONT VIEW

CASE JOINERY

For the most part, cabinet cases are assembled with simple joints — rabbets, dadoes, and grooves — that are fastened with glue, screws, and nails. Some cases include web frames (to support drawers) and face frames (traditional cabinets only). Web frame members are normally joined with tongues and grooves. Face frame members may be joined with lap joints, dowels, biscuits, or "pocket" screws.

MAKING RABBETS, DADOES, AND GROOVES

Of the many tools for making simple case joinery, the two best suited to cabinetmaking are the *dado cutter*

and the *router*. The dado cutter mounts to the arbor of a table saw, and can be adjusted to cut a rabbet, dado, or groove between ¼ inch and ¹³/₁₆ inch wide. The router must be outfitted with a straight bit to cut the same joints. These bits are commonly available in diameters between ¹/₁₆ inch and 1 inch.

The techniques for making rabbets, dadoes, and grooves are straightforward no matter what tool you use — set up the tool to cut a kerf of the desired width and depth, then make the cut using a fence to guide the stock or a straightedge to guide the tool. Always cut a few test pieces to check your setup before cutting good stock.

(continued on page 52)

PLYWOOD CUTTING AIDS

Although cutting sheet materials with an ordinary circular saw or table saw is awkward and difficult, you can make several simple jigs to make this job easier, quicker, and more accurate.

The *Knockdown Plywood Cutting Grid* supports the work. It consists of two 4-foot-long sawhorses and two 8-foot-long crossties. Each sawhorse has two rails for additional strength. The crossties rest in notches in these rails, forming a grid that will hold full-size sheets of plywood and particleboard. This arrangement provides better support than ordinary sawhorses, but does not require as much storage space as a more substantial cutting table.

The *Circular Saw Guide* enables you to make perfectly straight cuts with a hand-held circular saw.

The straightedge guides the saw, while the base makes it easy to position the straightedge before each cut. Cut both parts from plywood, and use a *factory edge* for the guiding surface of the straightedge.

The *Trimming Guide* lets you make straight, accurate cuts at any angle without time-consuming machine setups. The fixed mount attaches to the table saw rip fence, holding the clear plastic guide over the saw blade. The edge of this guide is perfectly straight and parallel to the rip fence. Unlike other jigs, which often guide a workpiece directly, the *Trimming Guide* requires that you attach a straightedge or a pattern to the workpiece. The straightedge slides against the jig, guiding the cut.

1 **When cutting up sheet** materials on the *Knockdown Plywood Cutting Grid,* you should adjust the depth of cut on the circular saw just $1/16$ to $1/8$ inch deeper than the thickness of the material to be cut. This will prevent the saw from cutting deeply into the supporting sawhorses and crossties and possibly weakening the grid.

2 **Before making a cut, arrange** the plywood or particleboard so the grid will support *both* pieces after the cut is completed. This is especially important when cutting small and medium-size workpieces.

(continued) ▷

PLYWOOD CUTTING AIDS — CONTINUED

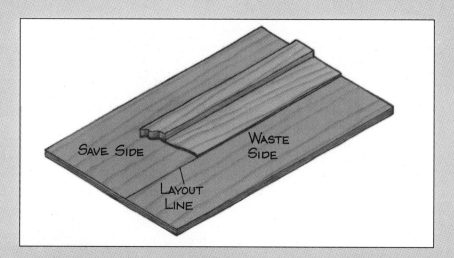

3 **To position the *Circular Saw Guide*** before making a cut, align the edge of the base with the layout line. Make sure the base covers the *save* side of the workpiece, not the *waste* side. When the saw guide is properly positioned, clamp it to the workpiece.

4 **Place the circular saw on the** jig so most of the tool's sole rests on the base and the edge of the sole butts against the straightedge. Make the cut, keeping the sole firmly against the straightedge. **Note:** Once you've used this jig with a particular circular saw and blade, it will only be accurate for that particular saw-and-blade combination. If you change blades or purchase a new saw, you'll have to make a new guide.

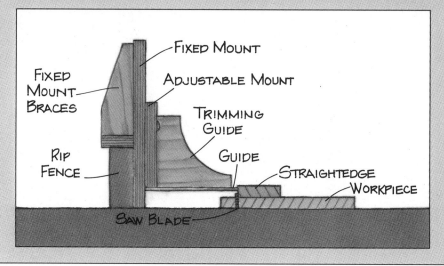

5 **To use the *Trimming Guide*,** attach the jig to the table saw rip fence. Position the guide so the edge is flush with the saw blade's outside edge (the edge that faces away from the rip fence). Adjust the depth of cut so the sawteeth will just clear the workpiece as they cut, then adjust the height of the guide ⅛ to ¼ inch above the saw blade. Using double-faced carpet tape, attach a straightedge to the workpiece along the layout line you want to cut. This straightedge should be at least ¼ inch thick.

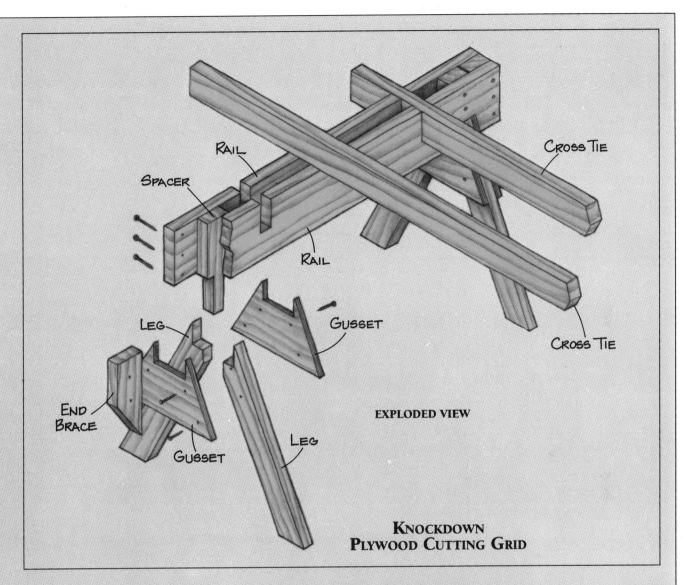

RAIL

SPACER

CROSS TIE

RAIL

GUSSET

LEG

EXPLODED VIEW

CROSS TIE

END
BRACE

GUSSET

LEG

**KNOCKDOWN
PLYWOOD CUTTING GRID**

6 **To make the cut, place the** straightedge against the guide and feed the workpiece into the blade. The workpiece should slip under the guide without touching it, but the straightedge must bear solidly against the guide at all times. After the cut, remove the straightedge from the workpiece. **Note:** If the carpet tape seems to hold the straightedge to the workpiece a little too well, use a small hardwood wedge to separate the two boards.

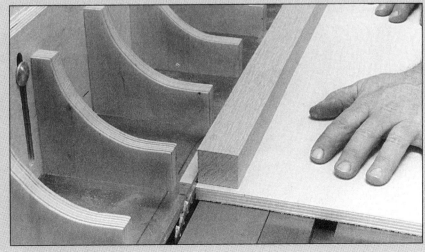

(continued) ▷

PLYWOOD CUTTING AIDS — CONTINUED

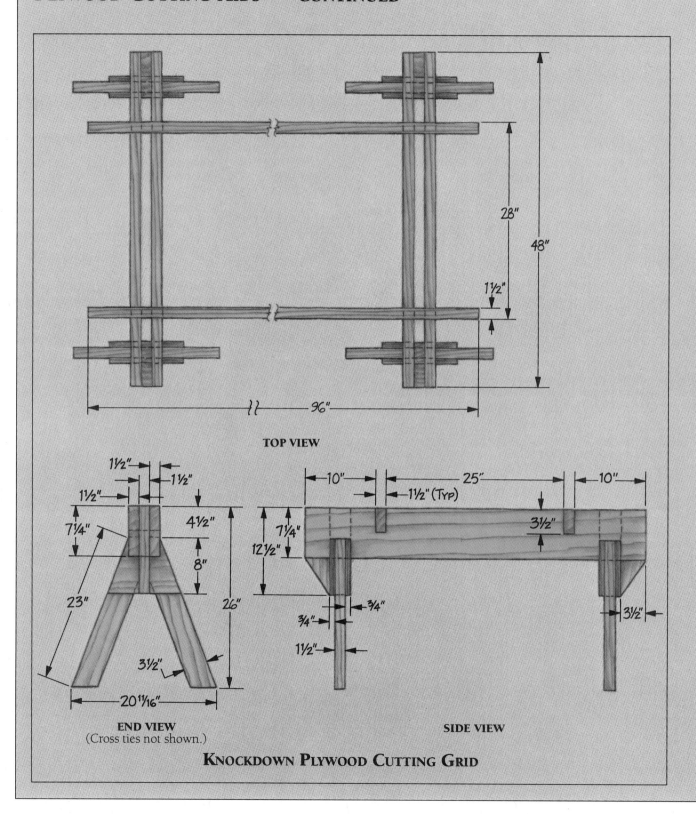

TOP VIEW

END VIEW
(Cross ties not shown.)

SIDE VIEW

KNOCKDOWN PLYWOOD CUTTING GRID

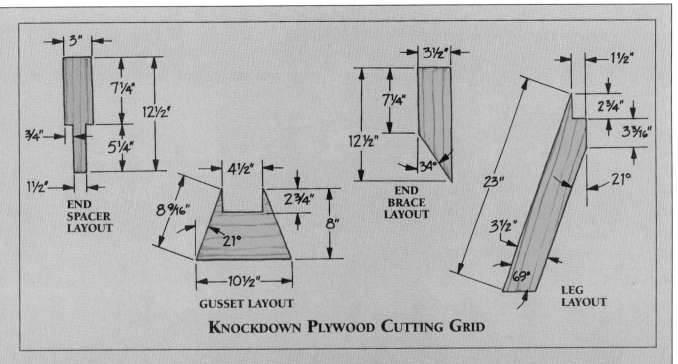

END SPACER LAYOUT

3"
7¼"
12½"
¾"
5¼"
1½"

GUSSET LAYOUT

4½"
8⁹⁄₁₆"
2¾"
21°
8"
10½"

END BRACE LAYOUT

3½"
7¼"
12½"
34°

LEG LAYOUT

1½"
2¾"
3³⁄₁₆"
23"
21°
3½"
69°

KNOCKDOWN PLYWOOD CUTTING GRID

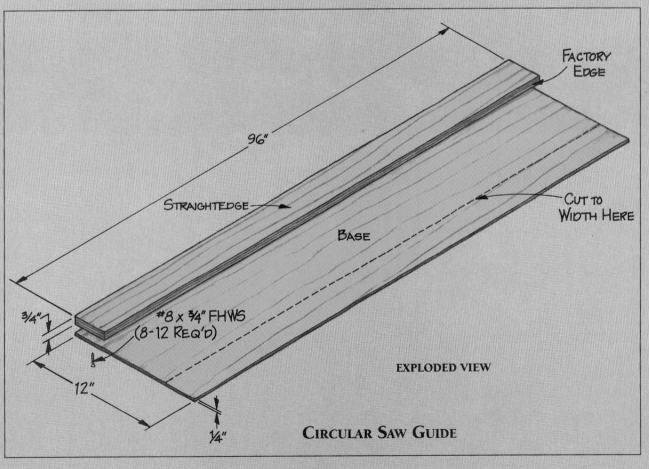

FACTORY EDGE

96"

STRAIGHTEDGE

CUT TO WIDTH HERE

BASE

¾"

#8 x ¾" FHWS
(8-12 REQ'D)

12"

¼"

EXPLODED VIEW

CIRCULAR SAW GUIDE

(continued) ▷

Plywood Cutting Aids — continued

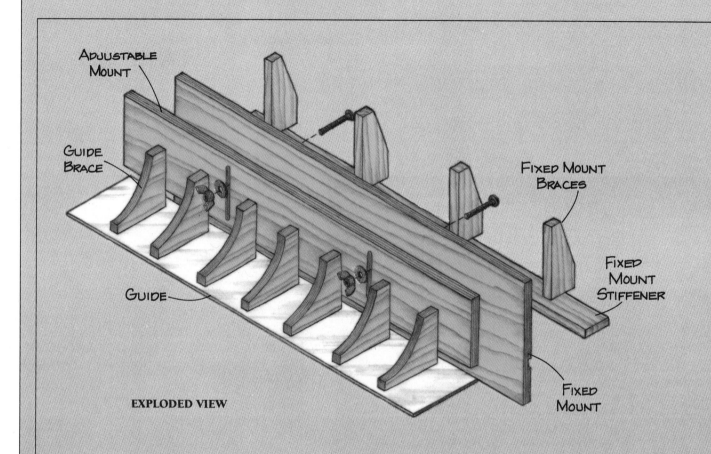

ADJUSTABLE
MOUNT

GUIDE
BRACE

GUIDE

FIXED MOUNT
BRACES

FIXED
MOUNT
STIFFENER

FIXED
MOUNT

EXPLODED VIEW

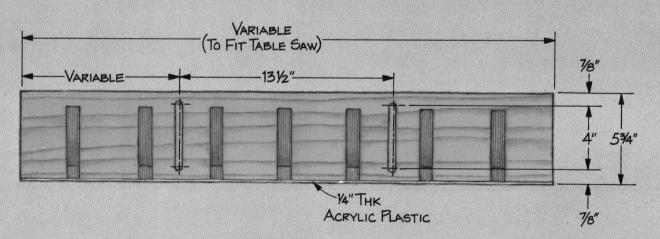

VARIABLE
(TO FIT TABLE SAW)

VARIABLE

13½"

⅞"

4"

5¾"

⅞"

¼" THK
ACRYLIC PLASTIC

SIDE VIEW

TRIMMING GUIDE

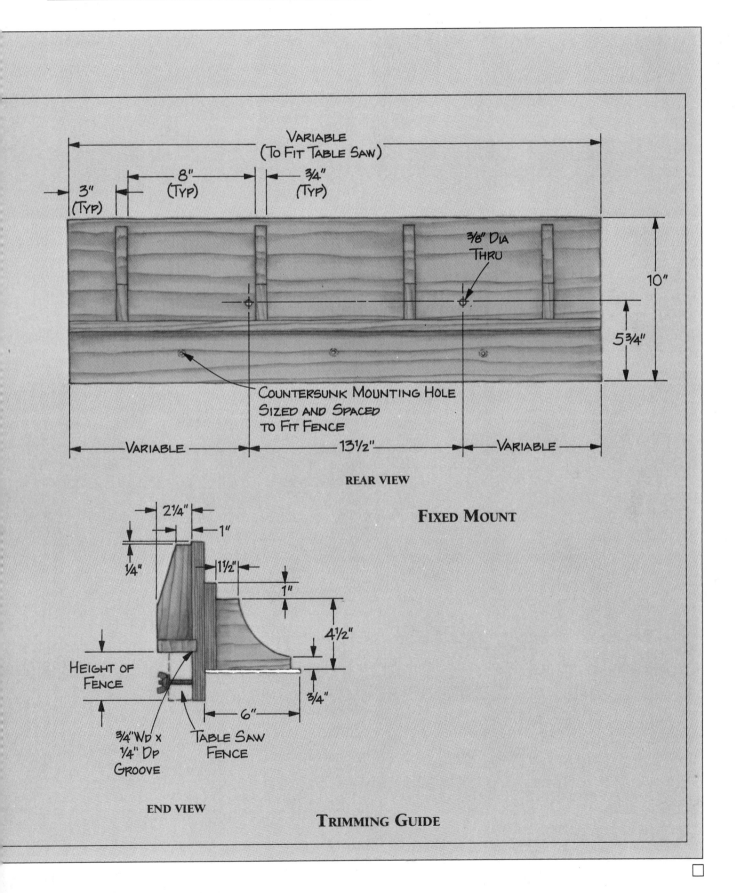

VARIABLE
(TO FIT TABLE SAW)

8"
(TYP)

¾"
(TYP)

3"
(TYP)

⅜" DIA
THRU

10"

5¾"

COUNTERSUNK MOUNTING HOLE
SIZED AND SPACED
TO FIT FENCE

VARIABLE

13½"

VARIABLE

REAR VIEW

FIXED MOUNT

2¼"

1"

¼"

1½"

1"

4½"

HEIGHT OF
FENCE

¾"

6"

¾"WD x
¼" DP
GROOVE

TABLE SAW
FENCE

END VIEW

TRIMMING GUIDE

A caliper with a depth gauge is handy for checking both the width and depth of rabbets, dadoes, and grooves.

There are, however, two special considerations when cutting these joints in plywood and particleboard. First, you must remember that the *actual* thickness of these materials is rarely equal to the *nominal* thickness. Measure ³/₄-inch plywood, for example, and you'll likely find that it's really ²³/₃₂ inch thick. If you're cutting joints to fit this material with a dado cutter, you may need a set of shims to achieve the proper width of cut. (SEE FIGURES 3-7 AND 3-8.) If you're working with a router, you must make two separate passes or use a special jig to guide the tool. (SEE FIGURE 3-9.)

Second, you must control the tendency of sheet materials to chip and tear as you cut them, particularly when using a dado cutter. A router leaves a fairly clean cut with little tear-out on the sides of the kerf. But a dado cutter butchers the plywood veneer, especially when cutting across the veneer grain. To prevent this, purchase dado cutters made especially for sheet materials. Or, use the same technique that was recommended to reduce saw blade tear-out — *score* the sides of the kerf before cutting the joint. (SEE FIGURE 3-10.)

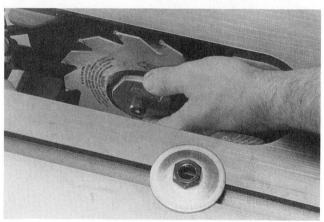

3-7 Carefully measure the thickness of plywood and particleboard before cutting dadoes and grooves to fit it — the sheets are usually about ¹/₃₂ inch thinner than their labels would indicate. For example, ³/₄-inch plywood is ²³/₃₂ inch thick; ¹/₂-inch plywood is ¹⁵/₃₂ inch thick; and ³/₈-inch plywood is ¹¹/₃₂ inch thick. If you're using a *wobble dado* to make the joints, simply dial the thickness needed by turning the wedge-shaped washers. Wobble dadoes are infinitely adjustable between ¹/₄ inch and ¹³/₁₆ inch. Unfortunately, they are best suited for light work — they may slip during long, heavy cuts.

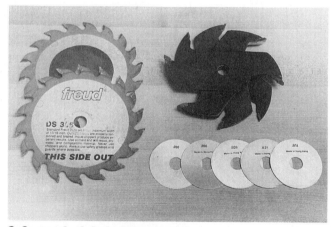

3-8 Stacked dadoes are better suited for heavy work, but you can only adjust the size of the kerf in ¹/₁₆-inch increments. To compensate, purchase a set of *dado shims* — large metal washers precision ground to several thicknesses between .010 (1/100) inch and .031 (¹/₃₂) inch. Place one or more of these washers between the chipper (two-tooth) blades to cut odd-size kerfs. For example, to make a ²³/₃₂-inch-wide dado, stack the dado cutter as if you were making a ¹¹/₁₆-inch-wide cut, but add a .031-inch-thick shim between two chippers.

3-9 Routing odd-size dadoes and grooves presents a problem similar to that of the stacked dado, since straight bits have fixed diameters and are commonly available only in 1/16-inch increments. To compensate, you must make the joint in two steps. Using a bit that's smaller than the kerf you want, rout a dado or groove. Then move the guiding fence or straightedge slightly and cut again. You can also use a special guide with *two* straightedges, as shown. Use one straightedge to make the first cut and the other to make the second. For plans and detailed instructions, see the "Adjustable Router Guide" on page 61.

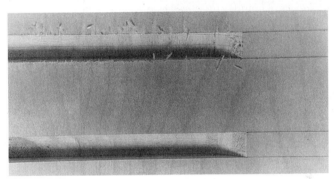

3-10 To reduce chipping and tearing when using a dado cutter, score the shoulders of rabbets and *both* sides of dadoes. The dado on the top was laid out with a pencil. The grain is badly torn where the cutter lifted the veneer. The dado on the bottom was laid out with a knife and is much cleaner.

INSTALLING FIXED SHELVES

The top, bottom, and any other fixed shelves almost always rest in dadoes or rabbets cut into the sides. However, there are two common variations on this joinery (*SEE FIGURE 3-11*):

■ If you don't want to see the joints at the front edges, use *blind dadoes* and *blind rabbets*. Notch the front corner of the top, bottom, or shelf to fit around the blind ends of the joints. **Note:** This joinery is never used on traditional cabinets (with face frames)

or contemporary cabinets on which the edge banding is applied after assembly — The face frames or banding hides the joinery.

■ For a more stable cabinet, assemble the shelves and sides with *rabbet-and-dado joints*. The extra shoulder on each end of each shelf helps keep the shelves square to the sides, and the construction resists racking.

FOR YOUR INFORMATION

There is another advantage to using rabbet-and-dado joints besides stability — you can compensate for the odd thicknesses of sheet materials without having to use dado shims or a special router setup. For example, if the shelves are 23/32 inch thick, cut 1/2-inch-wide dadoes in the sides and 7/32-inch-deep rabbets in the ends of the shelves.

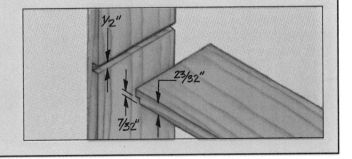

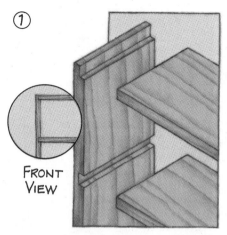

①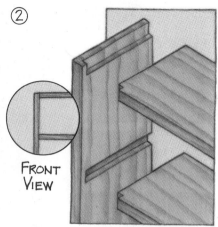

②

③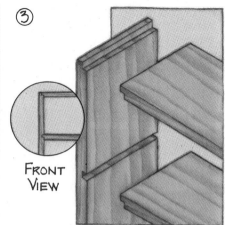

FRONT VIEW

FRONT VIEW

FRONT VIEW

3-11 There are three common methods of joining case parts in cabinets. Most horizontal parts rest in simple *rabbets* and *dadoes* (1) cut

in the sides. If appearance is important, use *blind rabbets* and *blind dadoes* (2). If stability is paramount, use *rabbet-and-dado joints* (3).

MAKING WEB FRAMES AND FACE FRAMES

Depending on the design of your cabinets, you may need to build web frames, face frames, or both.

Web frames support drawers, particularly large or heavy drawers. Join the frame members with glued tongues and grooves. (*SEE FIGURE 3-12.*) Using glue and

screws, fasten strips of hardwood to top surfaces of the web frames to guide the drawers. You may also need to fasten kickers to the bottoms of some web frames to keep the drawer immediately below them from tipping.

3-12 When you make web frames to support drawers, cut grooves in the edges of the *rails* (the frame members that run side to side) and matching tongues in the ends of the *stiles* (the members that run front to back). Glue the tongues in the grooves. If you wish, install *dust panels* in the frames — cut grooves in the edges of the rails *and* stiles, then slide plywood panels into these grooves as you assemble the frame. Dust panels are often a good idea — they keep dirt from sifting down into the spaces beneath them. **Note:** When making and installing web frames, you may also have to install *kickers* above each frame to keep the drawers from tipping.

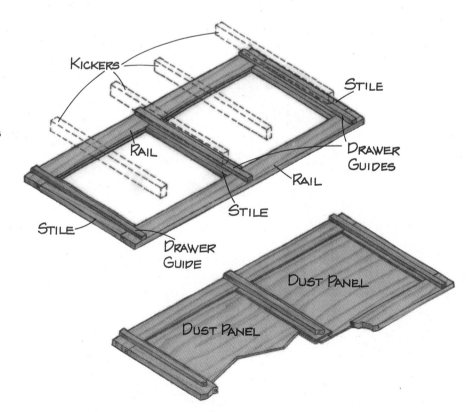

KICKERS

STILE

RAIL

DRAWER GUIDES

STILE

RAIL

STILE

STILE

DRAWER GUIDE

DUST PANEL

DUST PANEL

TRY THIS TRICK

Build the web frames slightly oversize, then cut them to final size on a table saw. Trim them when you make the fixed shelves for the cabinet. That way, they'll be precisely the same size as the shelves.

There are several ways to join face frame members. In previous centuries, face frame rails and stiles were usually joined with mortises and tenons. Recently, however, cabinetmakers have developed more expedient joinery. The two most commonly used methods are dowel joints and lap joints. Dowels are the easiest to install, while lap joints make a stronger frame. And there are two new methods gaining wide acceptance. As plate joiners and pocket drill guides have become more popular, cabinetmakers have begun to use biscuits and pocket screws to join frame parts. (*SEE FIGURES 3-13 THROUGH 3-17.*)

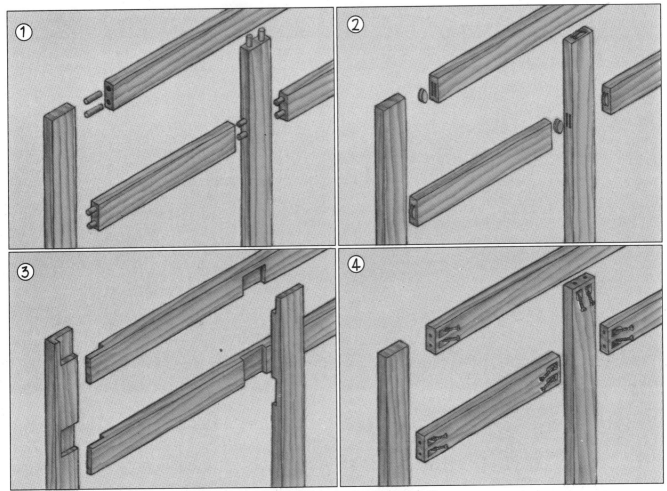

3-13 There are many ways to join face frame rails and stiles: (1) Drilling and installing *dowels* is, perhaps, the most popular method. Dowel joints are reasonably strong and easy to make. (2) Wooden plates or *biscuits* are as strong and as easy to install as dowels, plus they are more forgiving — you can shift a biscuit joint slightly as you glue it up. (3) If you need to make a strong frame, *lap joints* are a good choice. However, these require careful planning and measuring. (4) Of all the common joinery methods, *pocket screws* are the quickest to install. Unfortunately, they're also the weakest.

3-14 **To make accurate dowel** joints, use a *doweling jig*. This inexpensive tool helps position the dowel holes and guides the drill. Use two dowels per joint — this adds strength and keeps the frame members from rotating.

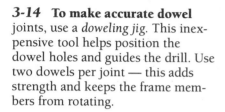

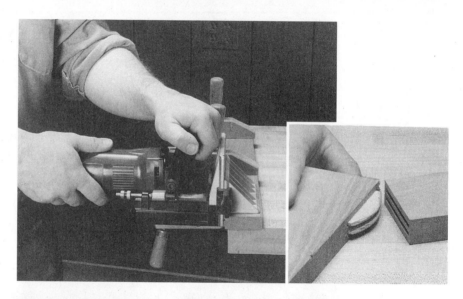

3-15 **Use a plate joiner or** *biscuit joiner* to cut grooves in frame members for biscuits. Install two biscuits per joint for added strength. If the biscuits are longer than the frame members are wide, you will have to file the biscuits flush with the frame members after assembling the frame.

3-16 **Make lap joints in frame** members with a *dado cutter* or *router.* When routing laps, either use the "Adjustable Router Guide" (see page 61) to control the router or make a simple U-shaped jig, as shown. Don't cut the laps on the end stiles through to the outside edge; otherwise, you'll see the ends of the rails on the completed face frame. Instead, make the end laps *blind* and cut the blind corners square with a chisel.

3-17 The quickest way to make the pockets for pocket screws is with a *pocket drill* and *drill guide*. The drill cuts both the pocket hole and screw hole in one operation, while the metal guide is clamped to the stock and keeps the drill at the proper angle. Drill these holes on the back faces of the frame members so they won't show after the assembled frame is attached to the case. For plans on how to make a "Pocket Hole Jig" that automatically positions and clamps the drill guide to the stock, see page 64.

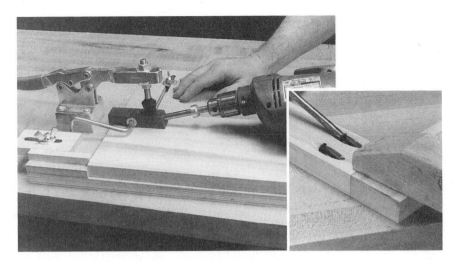

MOUNTING DRAWER BRACKETS

If the drawers will be supported on L-shaped brackets, there are several ways to mount the brackets in the case. Perhaps the easiest is to screw them to the cabinet sides. If necessary, place a spacer between the drawer bracket and the side. You can also dowel the ends of the bracket to a horizontal strip at the back of the cabinet (the nailing strip may serve) and the face frame at the front. (*See Figure 3-18.*)

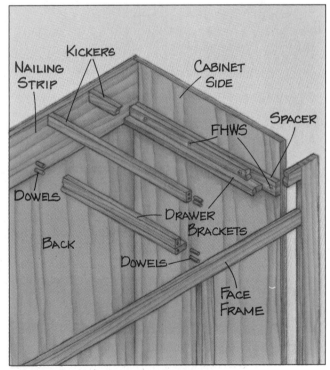

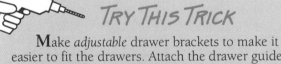

TRY THIS TRICK

Make *adjustable* drawer brackets to make it easier to fit the drawers. Attach the drawer guides to the bracket supports with roundhead wood screws and flat washers. (Do *not* glue them in place.) Make slotted holes for the screw shafts in the supports so you can move the guides from side to side about ¼ inch. This trick also works when mounting drawer guides to web frames.

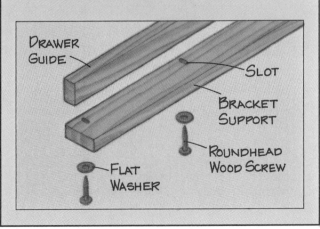

3-18 To mount a drawer bracket in a case, screw it to the cabinet side. In some instances, you may have to insert a spacer between the bracket and the side. If you can't screw a bracket to the side, add a horizontal strip at the back of the cabinet. (If the nailing strip is wide enough, use it instead.) Attach the bracket to the back strip and the face frame with dowels. **Note:** Like web frames, drawer brackets may require kickers.

INSTALLING EDGE BANDING

As described previously, contemporary cabinets don't require face frames. Instead, the front edges of the case parts (sometimes called the "finished" edges) are *banded* to hide the plies or particleboard. There are several ways to do this banding.

Strips of hardwood, 1/8 to 1/4 inch thick, make durable bands when glued to front edges of the sides and shelves. (SEE FIGURES 3-19 AND 3-20.) Some cabinet-makers prefer to make T-shaped wooden bands, installing them in grooves in the edges of the case parts. (SEE FIGURE 3-21.) These T-shaped bands are stronger than simple strips, particularly if the cabinets will see heavy use. But for most applications, strips are sufficient. Hardwood strips and T-shaped bands are usually applied *before* the cabinet cases are assembled.

3-20 After removing the masking tape, trim the banding to the proper width. You can do this with a scraper, a sander, or a plane, but you risk cutting through the thin plywood veneer near the banded edges. Instead, use a small router outfitted with a "Flush Trim Router Base." For plans on how to make this special router base, see page 68.

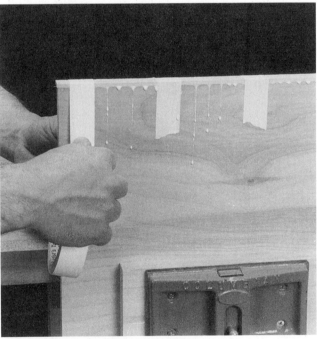

3-19 To make durable banding for the front edges of contemporary cabinet parts, cut hardwood strips 1/8 to 1/4 inch thick, and 1/32 to 1/16 inch wider than needed. Apply glue to the plywood or particleboard edges, then secure the bands with strips of masking tape. (Masking tape is slightly elastic, and multiple strips will "clamp" each banding in place while the glue sets.) You can also tack the banding in place with wire brads. The banding should overhang the faces of the cabinet parts slightly.

3-21 If the banding must stand up to heavy use, make T-shaped hardwood strips. Rout or saw a groove in the front edge of each case part, then glue the base of the T in the groove. **Note:** Commercially manufactured T-shaped bandings, made from hardwood or plastic, are available from many woodworking suppliers.

TRY THIS TRICK

Glue the edge bands to the front edges of the cabinet parts *before* cutting them to their final size. Then trim the *back* edges (opposite the banded edges).

You can also use strips of veneer or plastic laminate to band the edges. (*SEE FIGURE 3-22.*) Because they are so much thinner than hardwood strips and T-shaped bands, these materials aren't as durable. But they are somewhat easier to apply, especially if you do the banding *after* assembling the case.

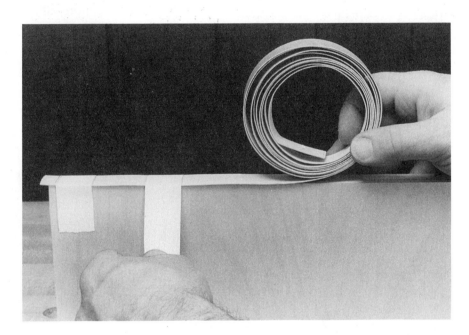

3-22 You can also band the edges of sheet materials with strips of veneer or laminate. Several companies manufacture rolls of paper-backed veneer especially for this purpose. Apply the veneer with glue and masking tape. After the glue dries, remove the masking tape and trim the banding with a knife or chisel. For instructions on how to apply laminate banding, see "Working with Laminates" on page 91.

CASE ASSEMBLY

DRY ASSEMBLY

When all the parts are sized and the joinery is cut, assemble the cabinet cases. Always begin with a *dry assembly* — assemble the case parts without glue or nails. Clamp the parts together or, if you intend to reinforce the joints with wood screws, screw them together. Just make sure that you can remove the fasteners and disassemble the parts afterward.

As you put the cases together for the first time, fit the joints. The parts must go together easily with a minimum of slop, yet there should be enough room for glue. If a joint is too tight, remove some stock from the appropriate member. If it's too loose, attach a shim.

Once a case is assembled and you're satisfied with the fit of the joints, take it apart. Finish sand all the outside surfaces. You'll find it easier to do most of the sanding now, while the case is disassembled, rather than waiting until after you've put it together.

TRY THIS TRICK

Before you sand, apply tape to joining surfaces to keep from ruining the fit of the joints. For example, if you sand stock from the ends of a shelf, it may fit sloppily in its dadoes. Put masking tape on the shelf ends to prevent this.

SUBASSEMBLY

When all the parts are properly fitted, assemble the face frames and web frames. Also, glue wooden cleats and hardware mounting blocks in place. It will be much easier to attach many of these small parts now than after the cabinets are assembled.

As you glue together each subassembly, constantly check to make sure the parts are square to one another. If these small assemblies are out of square, they may distort their respective cases. And if the cabinet cases are out of square, installing them will be a nightmare.

After the glue dries on each subassembly, sand the joints flush and clean. As before, be careful not to sand those surfaces that fit in dadoes or rabbets.

FINAL ASSEMBLY

Many of the major cabinet parts and subassemblies must be joined with glue, then reinforced with fasteners — usually flathead wood screws or finishing nails. Often, you must use both screws and nails to assemble cabinet cases. (SEE FIGURES 3-23 AND 3-24.) Make this hardware as inconspicuous as possible, hiding the heads as best you can.

Join the cabinet sides, shelves, nailing strips, backs, web frames, and face frames in this order:

■ Glue the top, bottom, other fixed shelves, and web frames (if used) to the sides. Reinforce the joints with finishing nails or screws.

■ Attach the nailing strips to the sides, driving screws through the case sides and into the ends of the strips. Or, drill pocket holes in the ends of the nailing strips and screw them in place from inside the case. If the drawers are supported on brackets, install these as you install the nailing strips.

■ Attach the back to the sides, top, bottom, shelves, web frame, and nailing strips. Some cabinetmakers simply fasten the back with finishing nails, wire brads, or both; others glue it in place, then reinforce it with nails.

■ If you're building a traditional cabinet, attach the face frame to the front edges with glue and finishing nails.

■ If you're building a contemporary cabinet and haven't already banded the front edges, apply the banding.

■ Let the glue dry completely, then sand the joints of the assembled case flush and clean.

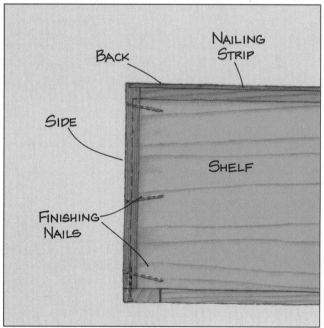

3-23 When using finishing nails to assemble the major case parts, drive the nails from the outside. Hold the nails at slight angles as you hammer them, and alternate the angles right and left (or forward and back) with each nail. This will "hook" the parts together, making it more difficult to pull them apart. After driving all the nails, set the heads slightly below the surface and cover them with putty.

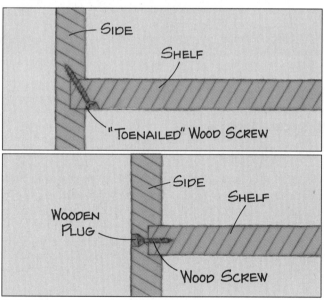

3-24 When using wood screws to assemble cabinet cases, you have two ways to hide the screw heads. Drive them from inside the case, "toenailing" each screw through the shelves or web frames and into the sides. Or, drive them from outside the case, but counterbore and countersink the heads. Then cover the heads with wooden plugs that match the plywood veneer.

ADJUSTABLE ROUTER GUIDE

To cut a rabbet, dado, or groove with a hand-held router, you must attach a straightedge to the stock to guide the tool. The positioning of the straightedge is critical; it requires careful measuring to rout an accurate joint. To make an odd-size joint (some width other than the diameters of the available router bits), you must make multiple cuts, positioning the straightedge at least twice. This adds to the setup time.

This jig saves much of that work. It consists of two L-brackets bolted together. The short arm of each L is fastened at 90 degrees to the longer straightedge. This lets you use either bracket like a large square, automatically positioning the straightedge square to the edge of the stock. By using a spacer block, you can quickly position the straightedge the correct distance from the layout lines. If you need to make multiple cuts, space the second straightedge the proper distance from the first. Use one straightedge to guide the first cut, and the second to guide the last.

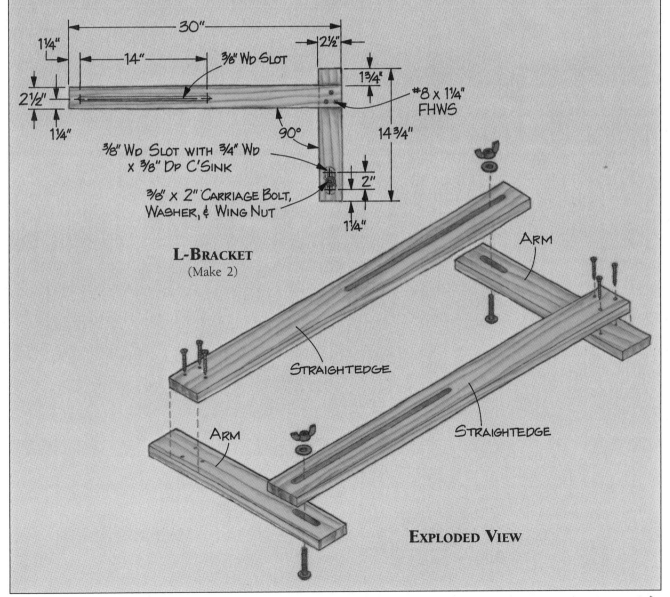

L-Bracket
(Make 2)

EXPLODED VIEW

(continued) ▷

ADJUSTABLE ROUTER GUIDE — CONTINUED

1 **To use the jig, first decide** whether you need to make one cut or two. If you're making a dado or a groove the same width as a router bit, you only need to make one cut. Consequently, you only need one of the L-brackets. Make a spacer block to help position the bracket on the stock. Figure the width of this block by subtracting the diameter of the router bit from the diameter of the router sole and dividing by 2. For example, to rout a dado with a $^3/_4$-inch-diameter straight bit mounted in a router with a 6-inch-diameter sole, cut a spacer block $2^5/_8$ inches wide: $(6 - ^3/_4) \div 2 = 2^5/_8$. Butt one edge of the block against the straightedge, then slide the jig along the stock until the other block edge is even with the layout for the dado. Clamp the straightedge to the stock.

3 **If you're making a dado or** groove that's some size other than the available bits, you'll need to make at least two cuts, using both brackets. Choose a router bit that's slightly smaller than the joint you want to cut, and bolt the bracket together so the straightedges are slightly farther apart than the diameter of the router sole. To figure the exact distance, subtract the diameter of the router bit from the width of the cut you want to make and add it to the diameter of the router sole. For example, to make a $^{23}/_{32}$-inch-wide dado with a $^5/_8$-inch-diameter straight bit mounted in a router with a 6-inch-diameter sole, space the straightedges $6^3/_{32}$ inches apart: $^{23}/_{32} - ^5/_8 + 6 = 6^3/_{32}$.

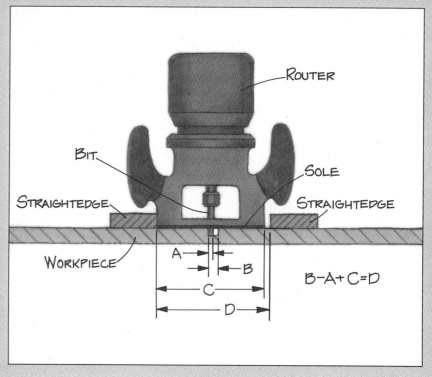

ROUTER

BIT

SOLE

STRAIGHTEDGE

STRAIGHTEDGE

WORKPIECE

A

B

C

D

B−A+C=D

2 **Rout the dado in several** passes, cutting ⅛ to ¼ inch deeper with each pass. Keep the sole of the router firmly against the straightedge as you work.

4 **Position the jig on the stock** using a spacer block and clamp it in place. Make the first cut with the router pressed against one straight-edge, and the second with the router pressed against the other.

POCKET HOLE JIG

A pocket hole is an ordinary hole, large enough to accommodate the head of a screw, drilled at an angle to the wood surface. This forms a "pocket" for the screw. At the bottom of the pocket hole, a second, smaller hole provides a guide for the screw shaft and threads.

A special pocket hole drill bit and guide makes it easy to bore pocket holes. However, the drill guide must be carefully positioned and clamped to the stock before boring each hole. To save setup time,

make a jig to quickly fasten the drill guide to the wood.

The pocket hole jig shown is designed to work with stock thicknesses between ½ and 1¾ inches. It can be configured to bore pocket holes in both the ends and edges of boards. As shown, the jig is designed to work with the Quick-Joint Pocket Hole Drilling Guide, but you can easily adapt it to other brands by altering the size of some of the parts.

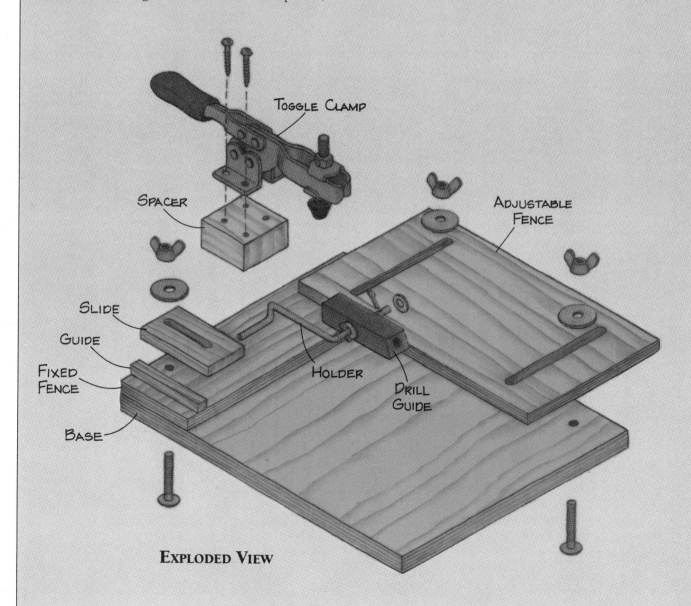

EXPLODED VIEW

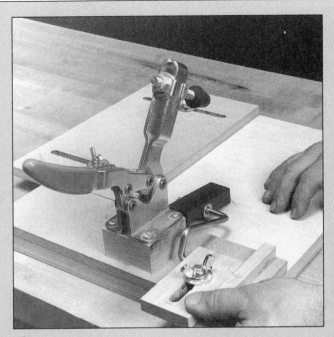

1 **To bore a series of pocket** holes, first adjust the position of the drill guide on the stock by sliding the guide holder forward or back. The front/back position of the guide determines where the screw hole exits the stock. Normally, you want it to exit midway between the two faces of the stock.

2 **To bore pocket holes in the** *ends* of boards, attach the fence to the jig and slide it right or left. The fixed fence holds long boards parallel to the drill guide and automatically positions these boards under the guide. To drill pocket holes in the *edges*, remove the fence completely.

3 **Once the drill guide and the** board are properly positioned on the jig, secure the toggle clamp. This holds the drill guide to the board. Set the depth of the pocket hole by fastening a stop collar around the drill bit. Insert the bit in the guide and bore the pocket.

(continued) ▷

Pocket Hole Jig — continued

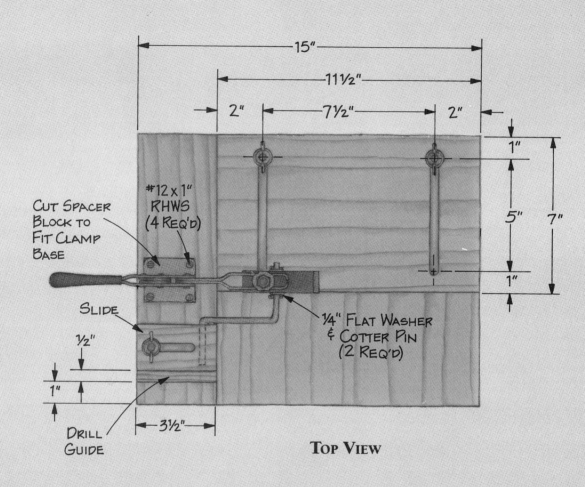

15"

11½"

2"   7½"   2"

#12 x 1"
RHWS
(4 Req'd)

1"

5"   7"

1"

Cut Spacer
Block to
Fit Clamp
Base

Slide

¼" Flat Washer
& Cotter Pin
(2 Req'd)

½"

1"

Drill
Guide

3½"

Top View

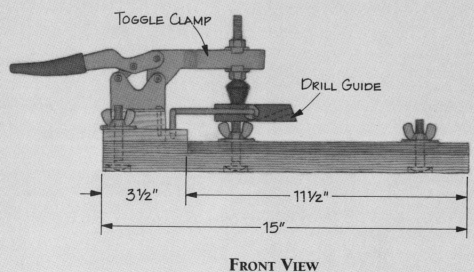

Toggle Clamp

Drill Guide

3½"   11½"

15"

Front View

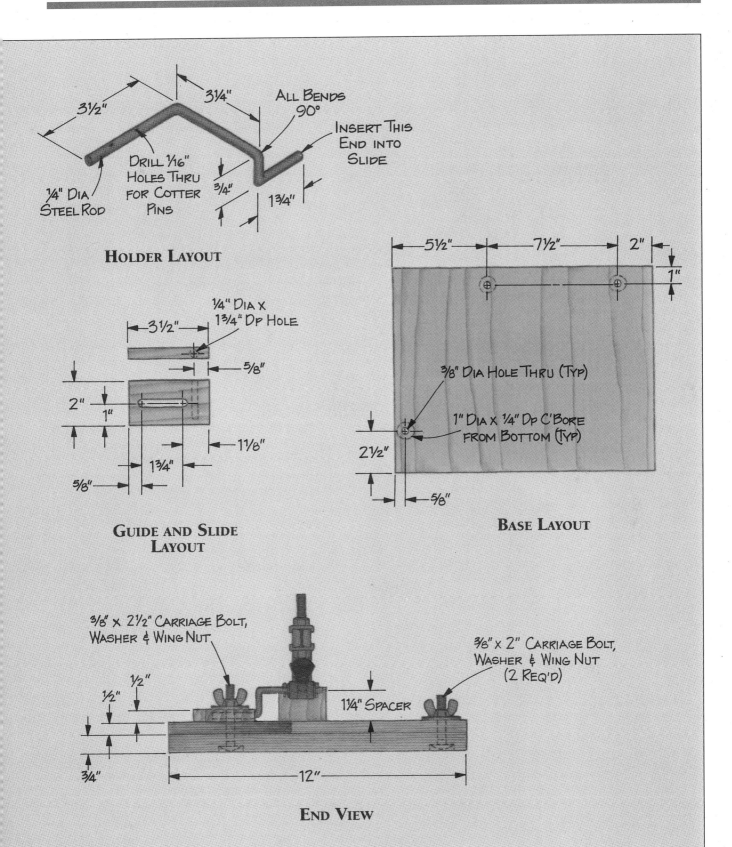

3½"

3¼"

ALL BENDS
90°

INSERT THIS
END INTO
SLIDE

DRILL 1/16"
HOLES THRU
FOR COTTER
PINS

¼" DIA
STEEL ROD

¾"

1¾"

HOLDER LAYOUT

¼" DIA X
1¾" DP HOLE

3½"

5/8"

2"

1"

1⅛"

1¾"

5/8"

**GUIDE AND SLIDE
LAYOUT**

5½"

7½"

2"

1"

3/8" DIA HOLE THRU (TYP)

1" DIA X ¼" DP C'BORE
FROM BOTTOM (TYP)

2½"

5/8"

BASE LAYOUT

3/8" X 2½" CARRIAGE BOLT,
WASHER & WING NUT

½"

½"

¾"

1¼" SPACER

3/8" X 2" CARRIAGE BOLT,
WASHER & WING NUT
(2 REQ'D)

12"

END VIEW

FLUSH TRIM ROUTER BASE

It can be tricky to trim banding and other cabinet parts flush with the surrounding surfaces. Trim a little too deeply, and you may cut through the veneer or laminate. To prevent this possibility, make a flush trim base for your router. This jig holds the router above the work, where the bit will cut off anything that protrudes above the surface. But as long as the router base remains flat on the work, the bit cannot cut into the surface itself.

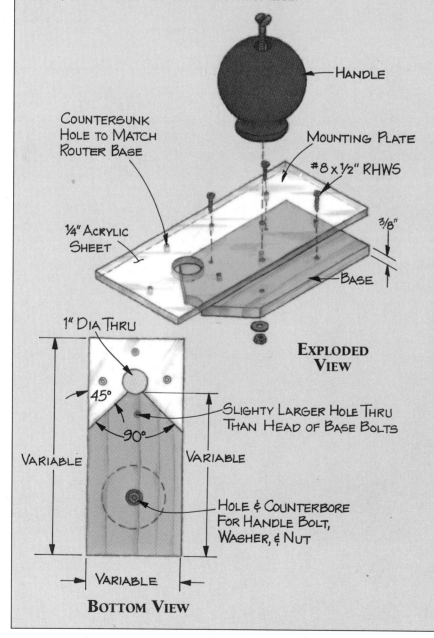

HANDLE

COUNTERSUNK
HOLE TO MATCH
ROUTER BASE

MOUNTING PLATE

#8 x ½" RHWS

¼" ACRYLIC
SHEET

3/8"

BASE

**EXPLODED
VIEW**

1" DIA THRU

45°

90°

SLIGHTY LARGER HOLE THRU
THAN HEAD OF BASE BOLTS

VARIABLE   VARIABLE

HOLE & COUNTERBORE
FOR HANDLE BOLT,
WASHER, & NUT

VARIABLE

BOTTOM VIEW

1 **Remove the sole from the** router and attach the flush trim base in its place. Mount a ¾-inch-diameter straight bit or mortising bit in the router, and adjust the depth of cut so the bottom of the bit is a paper's thickness *above* the bottom surface of the base. When you place the router on the work, the bit should *almost* (but not quite) touch the surface.

2 **Use the router and the flush** trim base to trim almost anything that protrudes a small distance above the wood surface. The most common use for this jig is to trim edge banding, but you can use it to trim screw plugs (as shown), veneer plugs, plastic laminate, surface repairs (wood or putty), inlays, dowels, and tenons.

4

DOORS, DRAWERS, AND SHELVES

Doors, drawers, and shelves are among the last items you make when building a cabinet system. And yet these parts are among the first items to consider when planning. The choices you make at this early stage affect everything that comes after. The arrangement of these elements determines the design and utility of the cabinets. The appearance of the door and drawer fronts helps define the style. And the way you install the doors, drawers, and shelves often dictates the construction of the cabinets.

Most cabinetmakers don't cut the parts for these assemblies until after the cabinet cases are completed. This allows them to fit the doors, drawers, and shelves to the finished cabinets — which may vary slightly from the original design.

MAKING AND HANGING DOORS

As mentioned previously, there are three types of doors — inset, overlay, and lipped. There are also three common methods for making doors — slab, board-and-batten, and frame-and-panel. **Note:** There are many more ways to construct and hang doors than there is room to show here. And not only can you make doors from wood, but also glass and other materials. If you want to get an idea of *all* the possible methods, page through the hinge section of a good furniture hardware catalogue.

DOOR CONSTRUCTION

Before you build a door, determine its overall size. This depends on not only the size of the door opening but also the *type* of door. (*See Figure 4-1.*)

■ An *inset door* is customarily sized ¹/₃₂ to ¹/₁₆ inch smaller than the door opening on all four sides. Many cabinetmakers prefer to build inset doors the same size as the openings (or a little larger), then trim them to fit.

■ An *overlay door* is sized differently for traditional and contemporary cabinets. On traditional cabinets, the doors normally overlap the face frame by ³/₈ inch on all four sides. On contemporary cabinets, the doors cover the front edges. Some edges are covered entirely by one door — this is referred to as a *full overlay.* Other edges are covered half by one door and half by an adjoining door — this is a *half overlay.* The size of a door depends on which sides are full overlays, which are half overlays, and the clearance required between any adjoining doors.

■ A *lipped door* is customarily ⁵/₁₆ inch larger than the opening on each lipped side. The rabbets that create the lips are ³/₈ inch wide and ³/₈ inch deep, so there is a ¹/₁₆-inch gap between the shoulder of each rabbet and the cabinet case.

From the overall size of the door, figure the dimensions of the parts, cut them, and assemble the door according to the method of construction you've chosen. There are some special considerations for each method:

■ When making *slab doors* from plywood or particleboard, check that the sheets lie flat with no cups or bows. If you're making the doors from solid wood, consider using quarter-sawn or rift-sawn lumber. This stock costs more than plain-sawn wood, but it has less tendency to cup. Whatever material you use, apply a finish to *both faces* — inside and out — to keep the wood from cupping.

■ When making *board-and-batten doors,* do *not* glue the battens to the boards, especially if the boards are three or more inches wide. When the wood expands and contracts with changes in humidity, glued battens will cause the door to warp or the joint to fail. Instead, attach the battens with screws or nails. Metal fasteners will flex slightly as the boards move.

■ When making *frame-and-panel doors,* glue the frame members together, but allow the panels to "float" in grooves or rabbets. (*See Figures 4-2 through 4-5.*) If you glue the panels in place, you will restrict the wood movement. The doors may warp, the panels may split, and the joints may pop. To prevent these problems, the panels must be free to expand and contract.

TRY THIS TRICK

When gluing up the parts of frame-and-panel doors, clamp them to a flat surface while the glue dries. This ensures that they lie flat on the cabinet fronts. The same trick also works well when assembling drawers and web frames.

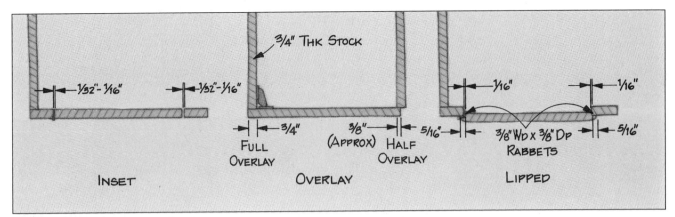

4-1 The size of a cabinet door depends on the size of the door opening *and* the type of door. In some cases, it may also depend on how the case is constructed and the hardware used to hang the door.

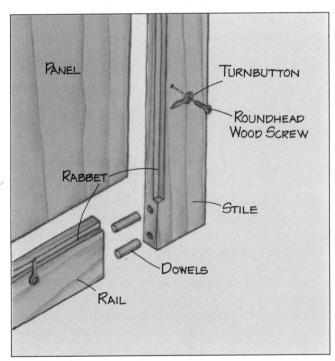

4-2 There are many ways to join the parts of a frame-and-panel door. Perhaps the simplest method is to join the rails and stiles with *dowels,* then rout a rabbet around the inside edges for the panel. Hold the panel in the rabbets with turnbuttons or wooden cleats. Although easy to make, this is not particularly strong joinery, and is best suited to light-weight doors that will not see heavy use.

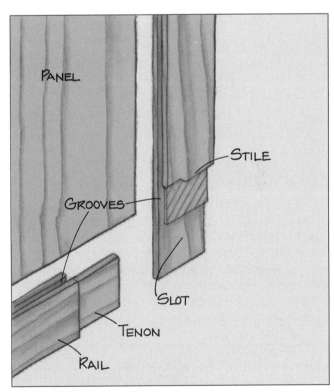

4-3 Cut grooves in the inside edges of the rails and stiles to hold the panels, then join the frame members with *bridle joints*. This construction is fairly strong and simple to make; however, the ends of the rails are visible on the edges of the assembled doors. Depending on your design, this may detract from the look of the doors.

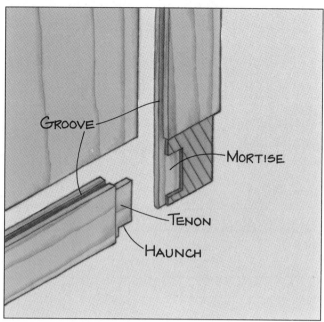

4-4 Cut grooves in the inside
edges of the rails and stiles, then join
the frame members with *haunched
mortises and tenons.* This is very
sturdy joinery, suitable for heavy use,
and works well for most designs. Of
the methods of door construction
shown, it is the most widely used.

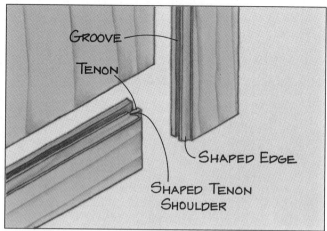

4-5 You can use a special set of
matched cutters for a router or
shaper to join door frame members
with shaped *sash joints.* Cut the ends
of the rails first, making tenons with
shaped shoulders. Then shape the
inside edges of both the rails and
stiles, cutting grooves for the panel
at the same time. Although sash
joints are highly decorative, the
tenons are too short for the assembled joint to be very strong. For this
reason, some cabinetmakers reinforce sash joints with dowels.

HANGING DOORS

To hang a door, you must first fit it to its opening.
Using a hand plane, scraper, or sander, carefully shave
the door edges until it fits the case properly. If you're
fitting a lipped door, use a bullnose plane or a rabbet
plane to shave the shoulders of the rabbets. Do *not*
plane the rabbet on the side where you will install the
hinges. If you change the dimensions of this lip, the
hinges may not fit properly.

> **TRY THIS TRICK**
>
> **T**urn the cabinet case on its back when fitting
> and hanging doors. The doors will lie in place as
> you work on them.

The method for hanging a door depends on the type
of door and the hardware you choose. Of the many
types of hinges, the three most commonly used in
cabinetry are butt hinges, surface-mount hinges, and
Euro-hinges.

■ *Butt hinges* are normally used to hang inset
doors on traditional cabinets. They must be mortised
(inlaid) into the case and door frame, and cannot be
adjusted once they are installed unless you plug and
redrill the screw holes. (*SEE FIGURES 4-6 AND 4-7.*) Also,
they are not as sturdy as other hinges. When hanging
an inset door that will see heavy use, consider using
wrap-around hinges. These look like butt hinges when
installed, but the hinge leaves wrap around the back
side of the face frame and door stiles.

■ *Surface-mount hinges* hang lipped or overlay
doors on both traditional and contemporary cabinets.
They require no mortise and, depending on the brand,
may be adjustable in one or two dimensions. (*SEE
FIGURES 4-8 AND 4-9.*) Surface-mount hinges for lipped
doors are sometimes referred to as *offset hinges.*

■ *Euro-hinges* (also called *European-style hinges* and
concealed hinges) are especially designed for contemporary cabinets, and will hang inset or overlay doors.
They can be adjusted in all three dimensions. Each
hinge comes in two parts — the *cup* and the *plate.*

4-6 To hang a door on butt
hinges, first mark the location of the
hinges on the cabinet case. Fit the
door to the case and wedge it in
place with slivers of wood or card-
board. Transfer the marks from the
case to the door frame.

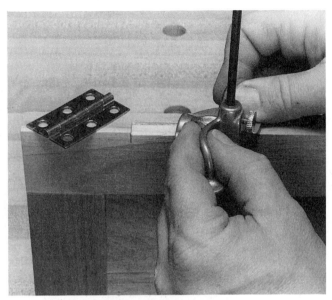

4-7 Cut mortises for the hinge
leaves in the case and door frame.
Each mortise must be precisely the
same depth as one leaf. Cut the
perimeter of the mortises with a
chisel. To cut mortise bottoms to
a uniform depth, use a router or
a router plane (shown). Drill pilot
holes for the hinge screws in each of
the mortises, install the hinges on
the doors, and hang the doors on the
cabinet.

4-8 To hang a door on surface-
mount hinges, first screw the large
hinge leaves to the inside surface of
the doors. You don't have to cut mortises to install the hinges; just attach
them directly to the door.

4-9 Clamp or tape the door in
place on the cabinet. Screw the small
leaves of the surface-mount hinges
to the case.

Install the cup in a stopped hole in the inside surface of the door, and screw the plate to the inside surface of the cabinet case. (*See Figures 4-10 through 4-12.*) **Note:** There are three different styles of Euro-hinges for inset, full overlay, and half overlay doors. The distance between the cup and the plate is slightly different on each style.

TRY THIS TRICK

When installing hinges and other hardware that must be screwed to a cabinet, use Vix bits to drill pilot holes. These bits automatically center themselves in the holes in the hardware.

4-11   Drill pilot holes for the hinge plates in the inside surfaces of the cabinet case. Several manufacturers of Euro-hinges offer special templates to help locate these holes precisely. Screw the plates to the case.

4-10   To hang a door on Euro- hinges, mark the locations of the hinge cups on the inside surface of the door. Drill a 1³⁄₈-inch-diameter, ¹⁄₂-inch-deep (135 millimeter by 13 millimeter) hole at each location. Most Euro-hinge manufacturers offer special drill bits for this operation. Insert the cups of the hinges in the holes and screw the flanges to the door.

4-12   With the hinge cups attached to the door and the plates attached to the case, slide the two parts of the hinges together and tighten the anchor screws. If necessary, use the adjusting screws to correct the front-to-back, side-to-side, and top-to-bottom position of the door.

MAKING AND INSTALLING DRAWERS

Drawer fronts are inset, overlaid, or lipped, and usually match the doors. Drawer construction varies, depending on not only the type of drawer but also how it's used, how it's installed, and the preferences of the cabinetmaker.

DRAWER CONSTRUCTION

A drawer is a box without a lid. Most have five parts — front, back, two sides, and a bottom. Some lipped and overlay drawers have a sixth part — a false front or *drawer face*. Drawers that are supported by web frames, drawer brackets, and bottom-mounted slides usually fit their openings with a $1/32$ to $1/16$-inch gap on three sides — top, right, and left. Those installed with side-mounted slides usually have a $1/32$ to $1/16$-inch gap at the top and bottom, and a $1/2$-inch gap at the sides to make room for the hardware. (The side gaps may vary depending on the brand of hardware used.) Lipped and overlaid drawer fronts cover their openings in the same manner as lipped and overlaid doors.

Unlike doors, drawers are usually built to the size needed or, at most, *slightly* oversize. It's much more difficult to plane a drawer to fit than it is a door, since you can't see how the parts fit when you slide the

drawer into the cabinet. The only drawer parts that are customarily cut oversize are the sides of inset drawers that will be supported by a web frame or drawer brackets. These often double as *stops* — when you slide the drawer into the case, they butt against the cabinet back or nailing strip, stopping the drawer so its front is flush with the front of the case. Cut the sides about $1/16$ inch long, then plane or sand them to the proper length after the drawer is assembled.

Cabinetmakers use a number of joints to join drawer parts. The bottom usually floats in grooves in the front and sides, and is slightly smaller than the space allowed so it can expand and contract. The back is dadoed into the sides. There are several ways to attach the front to the sides. This is the area that suffers the most stress as a drawer is pulled out of and pushed into the case, and the joinery is often chosen to withstand the anticipated strain. Here are three of the most commonly used joints:

■ The sides rest in *rabbets* in the front, and the joints are reinforced with nails or screws. (*SEE FIGURE 4-13.*) This is a simple, easy-to-make construction, but not particularly strong. It's best suited to drawers that will see light duty.

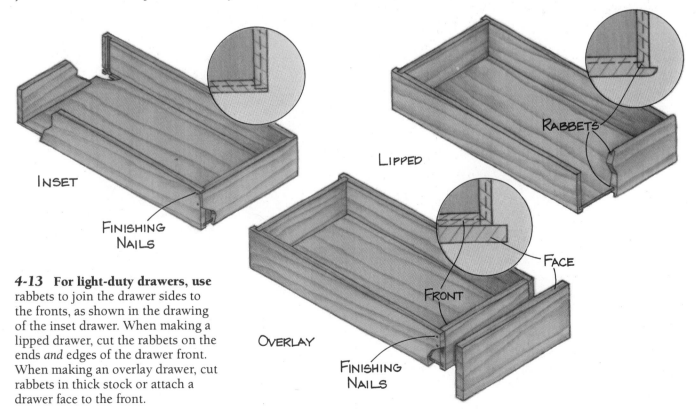

4-13 For light-duty drawers, use rabbets to join the drawer sides to the fronts, as shown in the drawing of the inset drawer. When making a lipped drawer, cut the rabbets on the ends *and* edges of the drawer front. When making an overlay drawer, cut rabbets in thick stock or attach a drawer face to the front.

■ The sides and front are joined with *half-blind dove-tails.* (*SEE FIGURE 4-14.*) This is extremely strong joinery, but it's time-consuming to make by hand, and it requires a router, dovetail router bits, and a special router jig if you make it by machine.

■ The sides and front are assembled with *lock joints* (also called tongue-and-dado joints). (*SEE FIGURE 4-15.*) This is a good compromise between strength and simplicity. Lock joints are fairly strong, and can be easily cut on a table saw or with a table-mounted router.

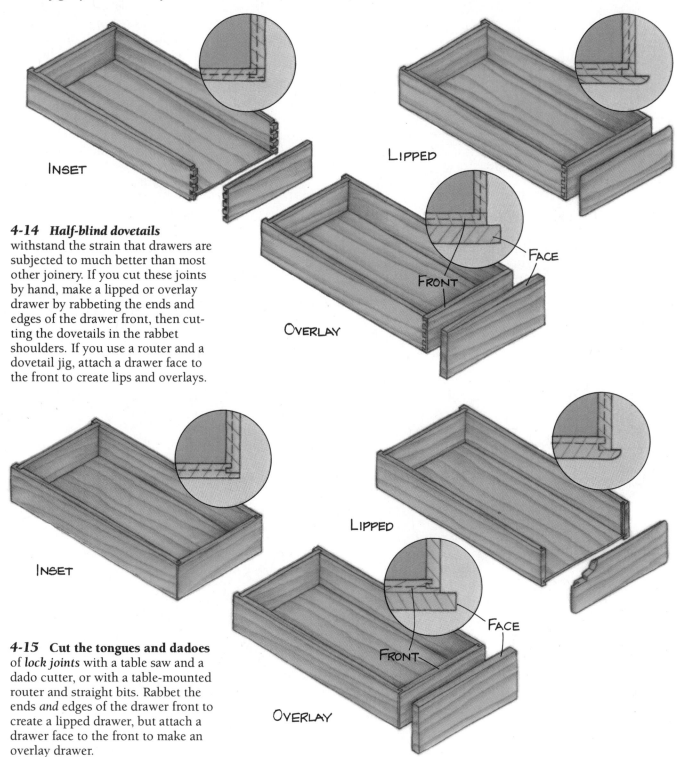

4-14 Half-blind dovetails withstand the strain that drawers are subjected to much better than most other joinery. If you cut these joints by hand, make a lipped or overlay drawer by rabbeting the ends and edges of the drawer front, then cutting the dovetails in the rabbet shoulders. If you use a router and a dovetail jig, attach a drawer face to the front to create lips and overlays.

4-15 Cut the tongues and dadoes of *lock joints* with a table saw and a dado cutter, or with a table-mounted router and straight bits. Rabbet the ends *and* edges of the drawer front to create a lipped drawer, but attach a drawer face to the front to make an overlay drawer.

Note: Traditional drawers are designed so you can slide the bottoms into the grooves in the sides and fronts *after* the other drawer parts are assembled. Nail or screw each bottom to the back edge. On many modern drawers, the backs are the same width as the sides, and the back is also grooved to help hold the drawer bottoms. All the parts are assembled at the same time. (*See Figure 4-16.*)

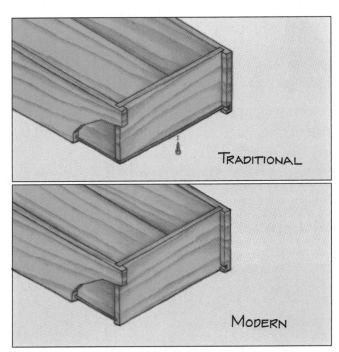

4-16 On traditional drawers, the bottoms rest in grooves in the sides and fronts, but are nailed or screwed to the backs. On many modern drawers, the bottoms rest in grooves in the fronts, sides, *and* backs. Which construction should you use? Whichever suits your fancy. Both designs are sturdy and let the bottom expand and contract.

FITTING AND INSTALLING DRAWERS

How you fit and install a drawer depends on how it will be supported. If the drawer will rest on a web frame or L-shaped drawer brackets, simply slide it into the case. Test the fit by sliding it in and out several times. If the drawer binds or sticks at any point, plane or sand the surfaces until it slides smoothly in and out of the cabinet. Or, if you have made adjustable drawer guides, shift the guides as needed.

TRY THIS TRICK

If you can't tell which parts of a drawer are sticking, rub the inside edges of the drawer opening and the drawer guides with chalk. Slide the drawer into the opening until it begins to stick, then pull it out again. Wherever you see chalk on the drawer, those surfaces are binding inside the case.

If you're installing an inset drawer and you've cut the sides long, plane or sand the back ends of the sides as needed. The drawer front must stop flush with the cabinet front when the drawer is pushed all the way into the case. (*See Figure 4-17.*) If you don't use the back ends of the drawer sides as stops, attach wooden stops to the web frame, the drawer brackets, or the back of the cabinet case.

If the drawer will be supported by side-mounted or bottom-mounted slides, the installation requires several steps. Begin by disassembling the slides. Almost all of this hardware comes apart in two pieces — one to be attached to the drawer, and the other to the case. Carefully locate the positions of the parts according to the manufacturer's instructions, and screw them in place.

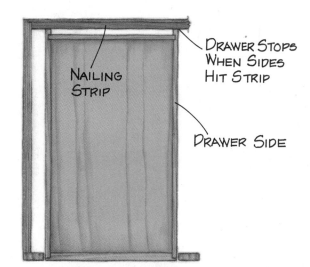

4-17 On lipped and overlaid drawers, the drawer front stops the drawer when it's pushed all the way into the case. On inset drawers, however, the drawer *sides* often serve as stops. Trim the sides so when they butt against the cabinet back or nailing strip, the drawer front will be flush with the front of the case.

Then slide the parts together again as you insert the drawer into the case. Test the fit by sliding the drawer in and out of the cabinet several times. If necessary, adjust the slides. (SEE FIGURES 4-18 AND 4-19.)

4-18   Most drawer slides have two types of mounting holes — round and slotted. When installing this hardware, use the slotted holes *only,* at first. Center each screw in its slot so you can shift the position of the slides slightly. Install the drawers in the case and test the fit.

4-19   If the drawer rubs or binds, loosen the appropriate mounting screw and reposition the hardware as needed. (Manufacturers customarily position the slots so you can reach them without taking the slides apart.) When the drawer operates smoothly, tighten all the mounting screws in the slots. Remove the drawer from the case, disassembling the slides. Install the remaining mounting screws in the round holes.

INSTALLING ADJUSTABLE SHELVES

Fixed shelves are considered part of the cabinet case, since they are fastened permanently in place. Adjustable shelves are not attached to the case, but rest on movable supports. By moving the supports, you can adjust the levels of the shelves.

ADJUSTABLE SHELVING HARDWARE

Three common types of hardware are used to support adjustable shelves. Each of these is recessed or inserted into the cabinet sides.

■ The simplest are various styles of plastic or metal *support pins.* Each shelf is supported by pins at its four corners. The pins rest in vertical rows of holes in the sides, spaced 1 to 2 inches apart. (SEE FIGURE 4-20.)

■ The sturdiest are metal *standards* and *clips.* Each cabinet requires four standards — long, vertical strips recessed into grooves in the cabinet sides. The clips fit in slots in the standards, each supporting one corner of a shelf. (SEE FIGURE 4-21.)

4-20   The variety of shelving support pins ranges from utilitarian to highly decorative. Most of them fit in ¼-inch-diameter, ½-inch-deep holes in the cabinet sides. A few European varieties require 5-millimeter-diameter holes.

■ The least obtrusive are *wire supports*. These rest in vertical rows of holes, like pins. The ends of the shelves are grooved to fit over the supports. When the shelves are installed, the supports are completely hidden. (*See Figure 4-22.*)

Note: Although all adjustable shelving hardware is installed after the cases are assembled, the required holes or grooves must be drilled or cut in the sides *before* assembly.

Try This Trick

When drilling holes for shelving support pins or wire supports, make a *drill guide* to help space the holes evenly. Drill a row of ¼-inch-diameter holes through a long strip of hardwood or plywood. Make alignment marks on the top and bottom of the strip to position the guide accurately. To use the guide, measure the cabinet side, making just two marks for each row of holes. Line up the guide with these marks and clamp it to the side. Using the guide holes to position the bit, drill stopped holes in the side. Not only does this method save layout time, it's more accurate than measuring and marking every hole.

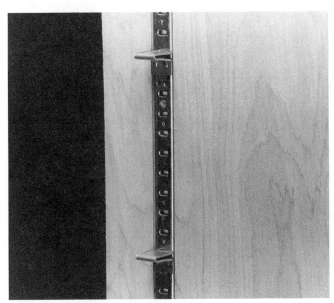

4-21 Shelving standards are recessed in vertical grooves, flush with the cabinet sides. The clips snap into slots in the standards. Standards and clips will support more weight than pins and are easier to align.

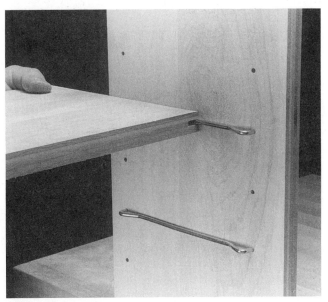

4-22 To install wire supports, you must drill holes in the cabinet sides *and* cut blind grooves in the ends of the shelves. When the shelves are installed over the supports, they not only hide the supports but also keep them from working loose.

5

INSTALLING CABINETS AND COUNTERTOPS

Up until this point in a cabinetry project, the label *built-in* may seem like a misnomer. In fact, built-in cabinets are rarely built in place; the individual units are assembled off site. Only after you've made the cases and hung the doors, drawers, and shelves do you install the cabinets in their intended location.

Many cabinet systems are installed in two steps. First, install the *units*. Decide how you will join the cabinets to the walls and ceiling — the methods differ depending on the structure of the building. Place the units in position, level them, and fit them to the walls if necessary. Then attach the units to each other and to the building.

Second, install the *countertops*. You may choose instead to install a countertop before installing the cabinet if the top spans only one unit. However, countertops spanning several counter units are best attached after the units are fastened permanently in place.

INSTALLING CABINET UNITS

METHODS OF INSTALLATION

You must attach the cabinets directly to the *structure* of the building. If the walls are made of masonry or concrete, bolt each unit in place using lag screws and expandable lead anchors. (*SEE FIGURE 5-1.*) If they're made of plaster or drywall on a wood frame, nail or screw the cabinets to the wooden studs in the wall. (*SEE FIGURE 5-2.*)

To locate the anchors on a masonry wall, first put each unit in place, fit it to the wall, and level it. Drill pilot holes in the nailing strips, aligning these holes with the lines of mortar (if there are any). Mark the position of the pilot holes on the wall and remove the units. Using a masonry bit, bore a stopped hole in the wall at each mark and insert a lead anchor in the hole. Reposition the cabinet units and drive lag screws through the nailing strips and into the anchors.

To locate the nails or screws on a frame wall, first find the studs in the wall. Mark the stud positions on the plaster or drywall. (*SEE FIGURES 5-3 THROUGH 5-5.*) As you put each unit in place, transfer the marks from the wall to the nailing strip. In some cases, you may be able to do this by sight; other times you must measure carefully. (*SEE FIGURE 5-6.*) Drive nails or screws through the nailing strips at the marks, making sure you feel them bite into the studs. If there's no resistance, you've missed the stud, so move the fastener 1 inch left or right and try again.

FOR YOUR INFORMATION

When locating studs, remember that in most newer homes (built in the last 50 years), the studs are placed 16 inches on center. In older homes, sometimes the spacing is inconsistent — the old-time builders often eyeballed the placement of the studs.

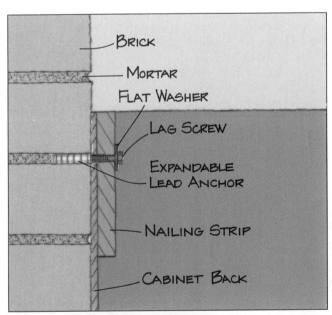

5-1 To attach cabinets to masonry walls, first install expandable lead anchors in the walls. If you can, position these anchors in the mortar between the bricks or blocks. (It's easier to bore anchor holes in mortar than in bricks or concrete.) Drive 1/4-inch-diameter lag screws with flat washers through the cabinet nailing strips and into the anchors.

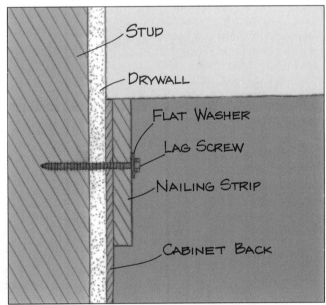

5-2 To attach cabinets to a frame wall, drive 16-penny nails or 1/4-inch-diameter lag screws with flat washers through the cabinet nailing strips, through the plaster or drywall, and into the studs in the wall. Most cabinetmakers prefer lag screws. Although they take longer to install, screws hold more securely than nails and are easier to remove.

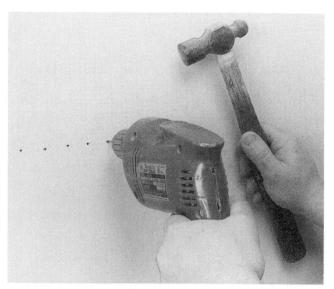

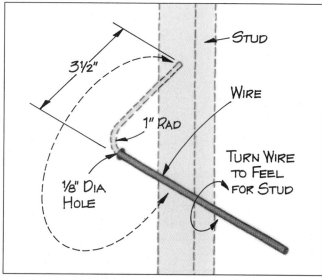

5-3   One of the most effective methods for finding studs in a frame wall is also the simplest — tap the wall with a small hammer and listen carefully. The tapping will make a low-pitched hollow sound over areas between the studs. As you tap nearer to a stud, the sound becomes more "solid" and the pitch rises sharply. Tap until you think you know where a stud is, then bore a small hole. If you don't find the stud on the first try, move the drill 1 inch to the right or left and bore again. Don't worry if you have to make several holes to locate a stud — if the installed cabinet doesn't cover them, you can fill them in with spackle. **Note:** You can also use this method to find joists in a ceiling.

5-4   If a stud eludes you even after you've bored several holes, bend a piece of stiff wire in an L-shape. One of the arms of the L should be no longer than 3½ inches, matching the depth of the cavity in most frame walls. Don't make the bend too sharp; it should have a radius of about 1 inch to allow the wire to penetrate the wall. Insert this short arm in one of the holes you've drilled, up to and including the bend. Spin the wire — if you feel it hit something solid, you've found the stud.

5-5   Mark the locations of the studs on the wall in pencil. Later, you can paint or wallpaper over the marks. If you don't want to mark directly on the walls, use *drafting tape* to show the stud locations. This material looks like masking tape, but peels up easily without ruining the surface beneath it. It's available at most office supply stores.

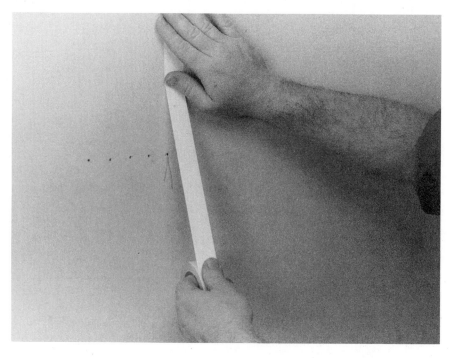

POSITIONING THE UNITS

Always install those units that rest on the floor (counter units and tall units) first, then install the units that hang from the walls or ceiling. This way, you can use the counter units to help support the wall units while fastening them in place. You can also make sure that the wall units are all spaced precisely the same distance above the counter units.

Start by removing baseboards and any other fixtures that might prevent the cabinets from fitting flush against the walls. Also remove the doors, drawers, adjustable shelves, and any hardware that isn't necessary to the structure of the cabinet cases. If you haven't done so already, cut the necessary access holes in the cabinet backs for plumbing and wiring.

Slide the counter units and tall units into place. If the cabinet sides or face frames must be fitted to the wall, push each cabinet against the wall where it will be attached. Using a compass, scribe the wall curvature on those parts where you have allowed extra stock for fitting. Cut the fitting allowance with a block plane, saber saw, or coping saw. (Refer to "Fitting Allowance" on page 35 for more information.)

The cabinet face frames or front edges must all be flush, and the tops must be level. The tops of the counter units must be flush, also. (SEE FIGURE 5-7.) If you need to raise the front corners of a cabinet unit, place small wedges or shims under the toeboard or bottom face frame rail. (SEE FIGURE 5-8.) If you need to raise the back corner, temporarily drive long hex bolts through the bottom to jack up the cabinet. (SEE FIGURE 5-9.)

If, after positioning the units, the backs don't rest flush against the wall, place shims between the backs and the walls at the stud locations. If these cabinets have face frames, and the face frames have a fitting allowance (that is, the frames overhang the sides slightly), put shims between the adjoining cabinet sides. (SEE FIGURE 5-10.)

Fasten the adjoining sides of the cabinets to one another with wood screws. Then attach the cabinets to the wall with nails or lag screws, driving the fasteners through the nailing strips and into the wall studs. (SEE FIGURE 5-11.)

Put the countertops in place or lay strips of wood across the top edges of the counter units. Place support blocks on the cabinets, then rest the wall units on the support blocks. (SEE FIGURE 5-12.) To install a wall unit that doesn't hang above a counter unit, use two or more *deadmen* to support it. (SEE FIGURE 5-13.)

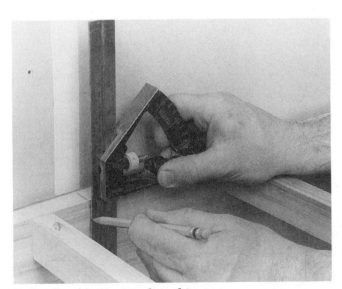

5-6 After positioning the cabinets, transfer the marks on the wall to the nailing strips in the cabinet units. For counter units, you can do this by simply eyeballing the marks. For wall units and tall units, measure the positions of the studs from the back corners of the cabinets, then transfer these measurements to the nailing strips. Remember to allow for the thickness of the cabinet sides.

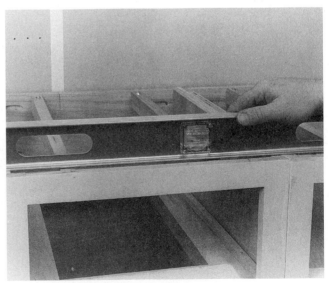

5-7 You must install the cabinets so the fronts are flush and the tops level. If you are installing counter units, the top edges must be flush, too.

5-8 If you need to raise a *front*
corner when positioning a cabinet
unit, place small hardwood wedges
under the bottom rail or toeboard.
Tap the wedges in place until the
front rises sufficiently. After installing the cabinet, remove the wedges
and fill in the gaps between the
cabinet and the floor with grout,
mortar, or a long wooden shim.

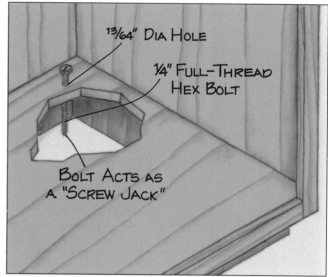

5-9 To raise a *back* corner, drill a
$^{13}/_{64}$-inch-diameter hole through the
bottom shelf near the low corner.
Temporarily drive a $^{1}/_{4}$-inch-
diameter, 6-inch-long *full-thread* hex
bolt through the hole. ("Full-thread"
means the entire length of the shaft
is threaded.) When the tip of the
bolt contacts the floor, it will raise
the cabinet. Turn the bolt until the
cabinet is at the proper height. After
installing the cabinet, remove the
bolt and fill the hole with wood
putty.

5-10 If the face frames of two
adjoining cabinets have a fitting allowance, place shims between the
sides. (The thickness of these shims
should equal the gap between the
cabinets.) Fasten the sides together
with wood screws, driving the
screws through the shims to hold
them in place. After the cabinets'
sides are joined, trim the shims flush
with the top edges of the sides.

5-11 If the back of a cabinet
stands out from the wall, place shims
between the back and the wall. Fasten the cabinet to the wall with 16-
penny nails or $^{1}/_{4}$-inch-diameter lag
screws, driving the fasteners through
the nailing strips and any shims.
Trim the shims with a chisel or a
backsaw.

Fit the sides and face frames of the wall units to the walls, if necessary. Shim the cabinet sides and nailing strips in the same manner as the tall and counter units. Screw the adjoining sides together, then fasten the units to the wall with nails or lag screws.

> ## FOR BEST RESULTS
>
> **Y**ou may find it easier to finish the cabinets *before* installing the countertops, particularly if you're using a countertop material other than wood. Do any necessary touch-up sanding to the surfaces of the cases, doors, drawer fronts, and adjustable shelves, then apply a finish.

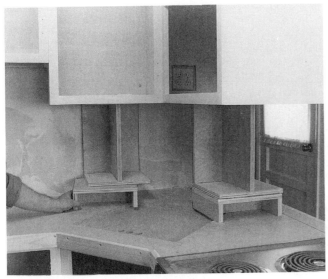

5-12   When installing wall units that hang above counter units, rest them on supports made from scraps of plywood. Each support should be sized to hold the cabinet at the proper level. If the wall units are different heights, make different sizes of support blocks. (See "Support Blocks and Deadmen" on page 88.)

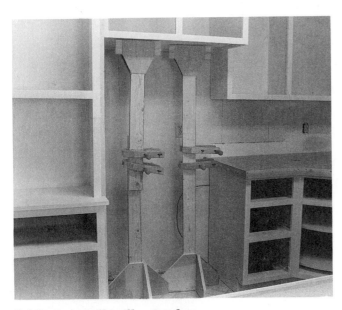

5-13   To install wall units that don't hang above a counter, make several "deadmen" from construction lumber and scraps of plywood. Rest the cabinets on these jigs while you install them. For added support, temporarily nail crossbraces between the deadmen.

INSTALLING COUNTERTOPS

COUNTERTOP MATERIALS

The best method for installing countertops depends, to a large extent, on the countertop materials. Your selection of a material depends on how the cabinets will be used and how you want them to look.

■ *Fiberboard,* backed up by plywood or particleboard, makes a good countertop for workshop and utility cabinets, where looks are unimportant. It does not stand up well to moisture or heat and is only moderately durable. However, it can be inexpensively replaced. (*SEE FIGURE 5-14.*)

■ Solid *wood* works well for almost any cabinet system, especially traditional cabinets. It's easily scratched and scorched, but it can be sanded and refinished to remove signs of wear and tear. However, it's not always the best choice for countertops that will be exposed to moisture, such as kitchen and bathroom cabinets. (*SEE FIGURE 5-15.*)

■ *Plastic laminate,* backed up by plywood or particleboard, is the most common choice for kitchen and bathroom cabinets. It's durable and resists moisture, although it scorches easily. Laminate is relatively inexpensive and can be installed with ordinary woodworking equipment. (*SEE FIGURE 5-16.*)

■ *Corian* is the brand name of thick plastic slab that looks similar to plastic laminate and has some of the same qualities. However, it's much stronger and more durable, making it a good choice for kitchen and bathroom cabinets that will see a lot of heavy use. Unfortunately, it's much more expensive than laminate. (*SEE FIGURE 5-17.*)

5-14 To make countertops for
workshop and utility cabinets, consider using ¼-inch *tempered fiberboard* or "hardboard" over a ¾-inch sheet of plywood or particleboard. (For a heavy-duty surface, use two ¾-inch sheets.) Don't glue the fiberboard in place; screw it to the backing material. When the surface becomes stained or worn, remove and replace the fiberboard.

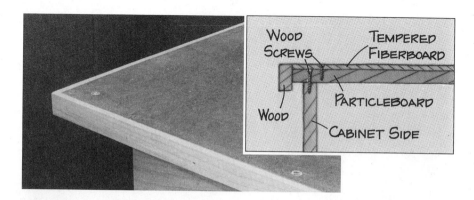

5-15 When making solid wood
countertops, it's often a good idea to cut the wood into strips and glue the strips together so the annual rings all run vertically. This arrangement is referred to as a *butcherblock* countertop. It's much more stable than wide planks glued edge to edge — butcherblocks expand and contract half as much as ordinary plain-sawn lumber and are not prone to warping or cupping.

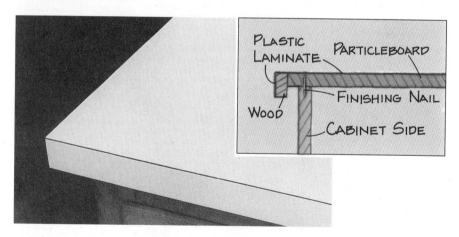

5-16 Plastic laminates are usually
very thin (usually between .028 and .05 inch) and must be glued to sheets of plywood or particleboard. "Plastic" is a misnomer; laminates are made of layers of resin-impregnated paper. Except for a few brands, only the top layer is printed with a color or a pattern. This is why laminates often show a light or dark line at the edge. If you chip or scratch the laminate, the color of the paper layers beneath the surface will show through the damaged area.

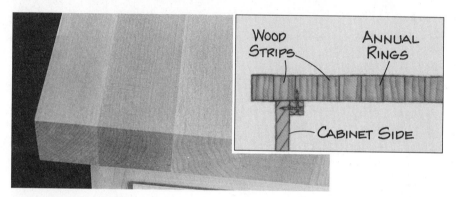

5-17 Corian is a synthetic
material which looks similar to plastic laminate. However, it's usually much thicker than laminate, and strong enough to be used in some applications without plywood or particleboard backing. On some kitchen and bathroom cabinets, the sink is molded into the countertop.

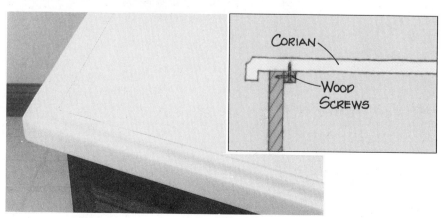

■ *Ceramic tile,* supported by plywood or particleboard, is a good choice for cabinets that will be exposed to moisture and heat. In bathrooms, the countertops and walls are sometimes covered with the same tile. In kitchens, cabinetmakers often set tiles in a small section of countertop next to the stove. This provides a place to set hot pots and pans. (*SEE FIGURE 5-18.*)

■ *Stone,* such as granite, marble, or slate, also resists moisture and heat. Food does not stick to polished marble and granite, and many chefs prefer these surfaces for rolling out pastry. But stone slabs large enough to use as a countertop are extremely expensive. Cabinetmakers sometimes install small pieces in strategic areas of kitchen countertops, as they do with tile. (*SEE FIGURE 5-19.*)

■ Thin sheets of *metal,* such as stainless steel or copper, backed up by plywood or particleboard, resist moisture and heat. These are sometimes used in kitchen, bathroom, and utility cabinets. Stainless steel is also a good choice for a finishing countertop in a workshop. Unfortunately, metal countertops must be custom fabricated in continuous sheets, making them very expensive. (*SEE FIGURE 5-20.*)

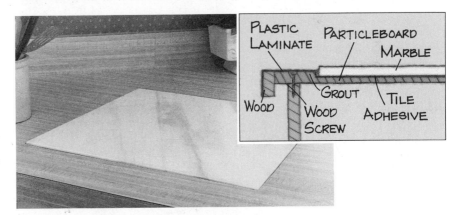

5-18 When using ceramic tile on a countertop, fasten it to plywood or particleboard with tile adhesive, leaving a small gap between the edges. Fill these gaps with grout. If you cover just a small section of the countertop with tile, you may want to rout a recess in the plywood or particleboard so the tile won't protrude too far above the surrounding surface.

5-19 You can set a small marble slab in a countertop in the same manner as tile — rout a recess, fasten the marble in place with tile adhesive, and seal around the edges with grout.

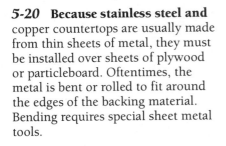

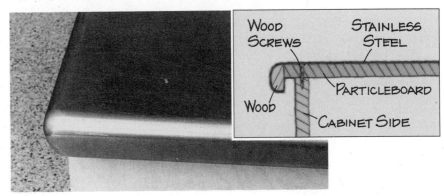

5-20 Because stainless steel and copper countertops are usually made from thin sheets of metal, they must be installed over sheets of plywood or particleboard. Oftentimes, the metal is bent or rolled to fit around the edges of the backing material. Bending requires special sheet metal tools.

FASTENING THE COUNTERTOPS TO THE CABINETS

Most countertop materials are installed over sheets of plywood or particleboard, called *underlayment*. The underlayment is usually ¾ inch thick, but it may be thicker if the countertop must stand up to heavy use. It may *look* thicker if the underlayment is trimmed at the edges with 1¼-inch- or 1½-inch-wide strips of wood. In addition, many countertops have 4- to 12-inch-high *backsplashes* along the back edges. (SEE FIGURE 5-21.)

Plan the seams in the underlayment so they won't fall directly beneath the seams in the countertop material. The rule of thumb is to keep the seams in the two layers at least 4 inches apart. Attach the underlayment to the top edges of the counter units with

SUPPORT BLOCKS AND DEADMEN

When installing wall units, you must rest them on sturdy supports while you position them. Even if you have a couple of strong helpers, it will be difficult for them to hold the cabinets steady at the proper level while you fasten the units to the wall.

If these cabinets hang above counter units, make *support blocks* from scraps of plywood. These should hold the cabinets at the precise level where you want to fasten them — you may have to make several different sizes, depending on the design of

your cabinet system. Each support block comes apart in two pieces — the base and the stand. This makes it easy to remove after the cabinet is installed. Slide the base out from under its stand, let the stand drop down, then slide the stand out from under the cabinet.

If the cabinets simply hang above the floor, make *deadmen* from two-by-fours and plywood to support them. Unlike support blocks, you don't have to build these to the precise height needed. Adjust the height to the desired level when you clamp the upper post to the lower one. To remove the deadmen after the cabinets are installed, loosen the clamps.

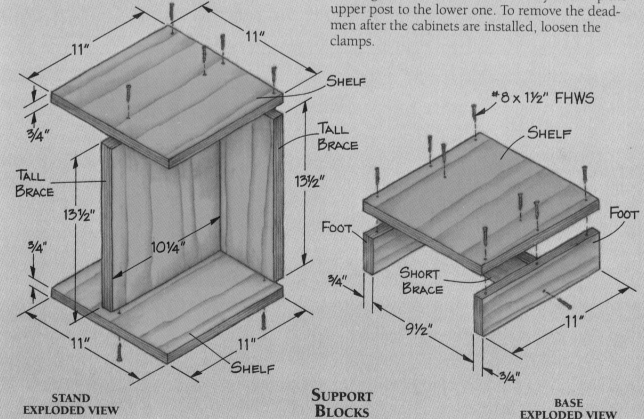

STAND
EXPLODED VIEW

SUPPORT
BLOCKS

BASE
EXPLODED VIEW

glue and finishing nails. Then fasten the banding to the front edges of the underlayment. (*SEE FIGURE 5-22.*)

If you're using ceramic tile or metal as the countertop material, attach the backsplash at this time. If necessary, fit the backsplash to the curvature of the wall. Fasten the backsplash in place, driving nails or wood screws through it and into the studs in the wall. Then cover the banding, underlayment, and backsplash with tile or metal.

If you're using plastic laminate, you have a choice. You can prefabricate the countertop, laminating the underlayment and backsplash while the counter is still unattached. Fasten the completed counter to the cabinet, then attach the backsplash. Or, you can do the lamination on site. If you choose the latter method, attach the underlayment and banding to the cabinets, then cover them with laminate. Fit the backsplash to the curvature of the wall and apply the laminate while

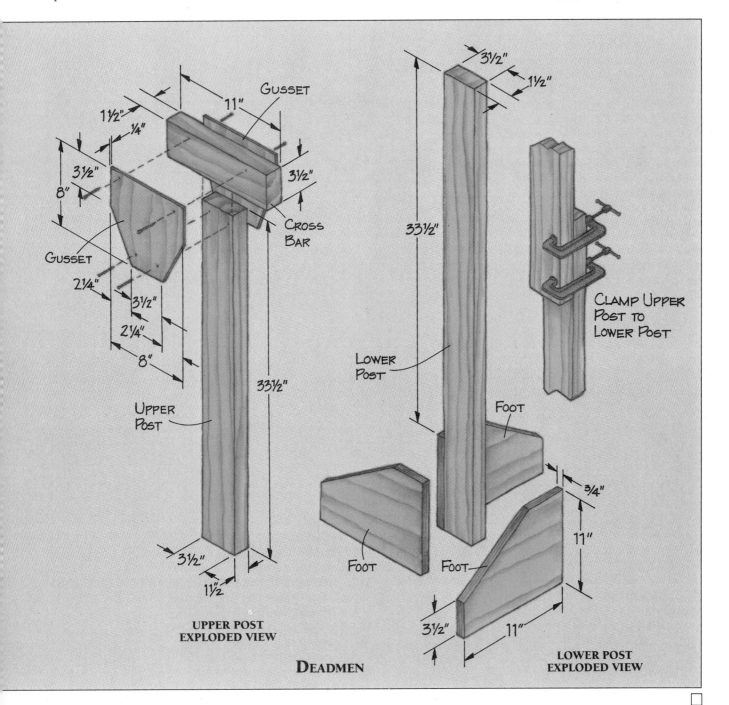

DEADMEN

it's still unattached. Attach the laminated backsplash to the wall with construction adhesive. (For complete instructions on how to install plastic laminates, see "Working with Laminates" on the facing page.)

If you're using solid wood, Corian, or a pre-assembled countertop, you don't need underlayment. Instead, fasten the material directly to the cabinets with screws. Install cleats at the top edges of the cabinet units, or drill screw pockets in the cabinet sides, nailing strip, and top face frame rail (if any). Drive the screws from inside the cabinet, up through the cleats or pockets, and into the countertop. (SEE FIGURE 5-23.)

Once the countertops are installed, apply a finish to the cabinets if you haven't done so already. Then reinstall the doors, drawers, adjustable shelves, and hardware.

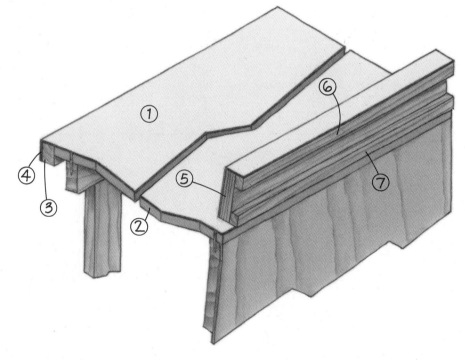

5-21 Most counter materials, such as *plastic laminates* (1), are very thin and must be installed over thick sheets of plywood or particleboard, called *underlayment* (2). The front edge of the underlayment is covered with wooden *banding* (3). This banding is often slightly wider than the underlayment is thick, and is covered with a vertical piece of countertop material known as a *self edge* (4). The *backsplash* (5) hides the back edge of the countertop and is usually covered with the same countertop materials as the underlayment and banding. If the wall is uneven, the backsplash may require a *fitting allowance* (6) and a *spacer* (7). Both the fitting allowance and the spacer must be cut to match the curve of the wall.

5-22 Attach the countertop underlayment to the cabinets, and the banding to the underlayment, with glue and finishing nails. Don't worry about hiding the heads of these nails; the countertop material will cover them.

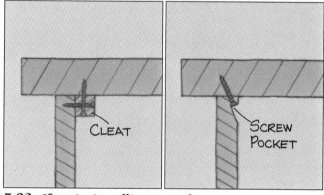

5-23 If you're installing a wooden butcherblock or some other material that doesn't require underlayment, screw the countertop directly to the top edges of the counter units. Drive the screws from inside the cabinets so you won't see them, using either *cleats* or *screw pockets* to anchor the screw heads.

WORKING WITH LAMINATES

Plastic laminates are arguably the most versatile of all countertop materials. They're well-suited for kitchen, bathroom, and utility cabinets, as well as some workshop applications. They are readily available at most building supply stores and come in hundreds of colors, patterns, and textures. You can purchase ready-to-install laminate-covered countertops in standard sizes, complete with finished edges and backsplashes. Or, you can make custom countertops, cutting and installing the laminate with ordinary woodworking tools.

If you install the laminate yourself, the basic method is very simple. First, cut the laminate sheet slightly oversize. Attach it to the plywood or particleboard backing with contact cement, letting the edges overhang the backing. Then trim the laminate to its final size with a router and a special trimming bit.

You'll find it's easiest to cut *and* trim the laminate with a hand-held router. (Many cabinet shops cut laminate to rough size with table saws, but these often have special blades and added support for handling thin sheets.) Make a *Laminate Cutting Guide* to help saw straight cuts in the material. This jig is similar to the *Circular Saw Guide* on page 49 and uses the factory edge of a sheet of plywood as a long straightedge. If you've already made a *Circular Saw Guide,* you can use it for both your circular saw and your router by routing a ³/₈-inch-wide groove in the base.

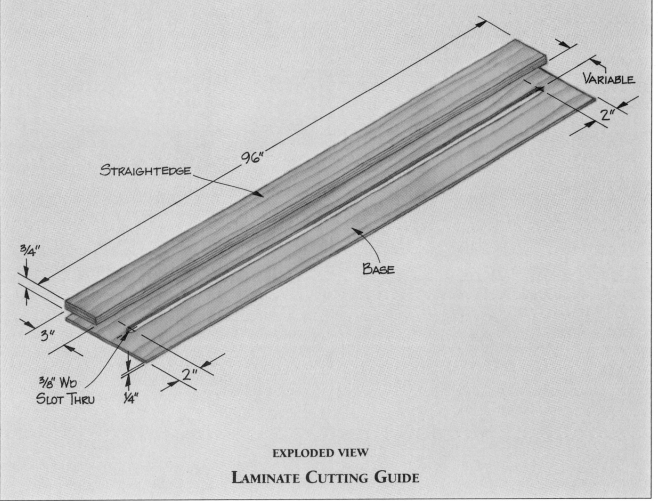

STRAIGHTEDGE

96"

VARIABLE

2"

BASE

3/4"

3"

3/8" WD SLOT THRU

1/4"

2"

EXPLODED VIEW

LAMINATE CUTTING GUIDE

(continued) ▷

WORKING WITH LAMINATES — CONTINUED

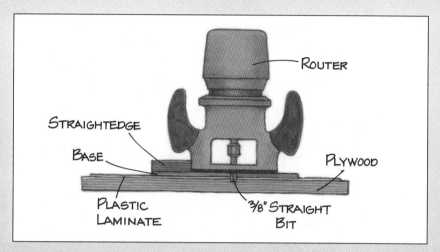

1 **To use the *Laminate Cutting***
Guide (or the modified *Circular Saw Guide*), place the laminate on a cutting table. If you don't have a cutting table, lay a sheet of plywood across the *Knockdown Plywood Cutting Grid* (see page 47) and lay the laminate on the plywood. Install a ³/₈-inch carbide-tipped straight bit in your router. (Ordinary high-speed steel bits dull quickly when cutting laminate.) Mea-

sure and mark where you want to cut the material. Clamp the guide over the laminate, lining up the appropriate edge of the groove with the layout line. Adjust the depth of cut so

the straight bit will cut through the laminate and about ¹/₃₂ inch into the plywood. Cut the laminate with the router, keeping the base of the router firmly against the straightedge.

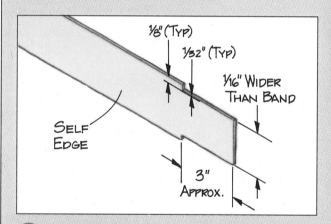

3 **Because a router can't trim**
closer than 2 or 3 inches to a vertical surface, notch the end of the self edge, as shown, where it will butt against a wall or tall cabinet. After you've attached the self edge to the banding, you can trim this notched portion with a file.

4 **Using a brush, apply contact**
cement to *both* the front face of the banding and the back of the self edge. Spread the cement as evenly as possible, but do *not* brush the same area twice. The cement dries very quickly. If you attempt to brush it out after it begins to dry, the cement will roll up in clumps.

2 **Begin covering the counter-** top with plastic laminate by attaching the self edge to the banding. (If you attach the self edge *after* you cover the underlayment, the seam will face *up*. Spilled liquids may soak into the seam, eventually causing the self edge to come loose.) Measure and mark a thin strip of laminate, about ¼ inch wider than the banding, and cut it with the router.

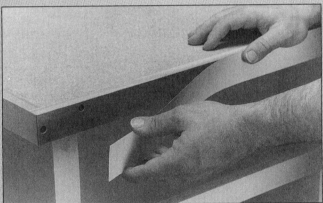

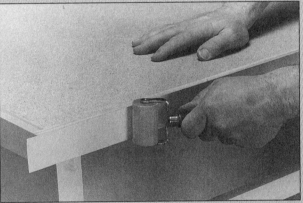

5 **Let the cement dry until the** surface appears dull (usually about 10 to 15 minutes). Position the self edge next to the banding. Make doubly sure the laminate is positioned properly! Once you apply it to the banding, it's impossible to move it, even slightly. Working from one end of the banding to the other, press the self edge lightly in place. If you must apply a long strip, you may need a helper to assist you.

6 **Using a veneer roller or a** rolling pin, apply pressure to the self edge. Press as hard as you can to create a firm bond between the laminate and the backing. However, be careful to keep the roller flat against the laminate. If it tips, it may crack the self edge where it overhangs the banding.

(continued) ▷

WORKING WITH LAMINATES — CONTINUED

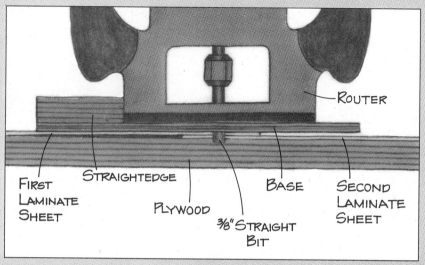

FIRST LAMINATE SHEET — STRAIGHTEDGE — PLYWOOD — ROUTER — ⅜" STRAIGHT BIT — BASE — SECOND LAMINATE SHEET

7 **Mount a *flush trimming bit*** with a ball-bearing pilot in your router. This piloted bit is specially designed to cut plastic laminate flush with the edge of its backing material. Trim both the upper and lower edges of the self edge. If necessary, file the self edge flush with the banding in those areas where the router won't reach. **Note:** If you use a bit piloted by a solid post, the wood banding will likely burn where the bit contacts it.

8 **Cut the laminate that covers** the underlayment ½ to 1 inch over-size. (You need a little extra room for mistakes when working with larger pieces.) If you must join two sheets of laminate to cover the underlayment, *joint* the adjoining edges. To do this, lap the two sheets where you want to join them and fasten them together with double-faced carpet tape. Position the *Laminate Cutting Guide* over the lapped area and clamp it in place.

Keeping the router firmly against the jig's straightedge, cut through *both* sheets with a straight bit. When you remove the guide and the carpet tape, the routed edges of the two sheets will match perfectly. Join the sheets temporarily with masking tape, sticking the tape to the *top* side of the laminate.

11 **When the laminate is** securely attached to the underlayment, trim the overhanging edges. For this operation, you can use a *bevel trimming bit* with a ball-bearing pilot, if you wish. This bit will trim the laminate to size and cut either a 10- or 15-degree bevel in the edge. A beveled edge feels softer and won't chip as easily. **Note:** Many cabinetmakers lightly file the seam between the vertical and horizontal pieces of laminate *after* trimming away the excess with a router. This polishes the seam and removes any burn marks.

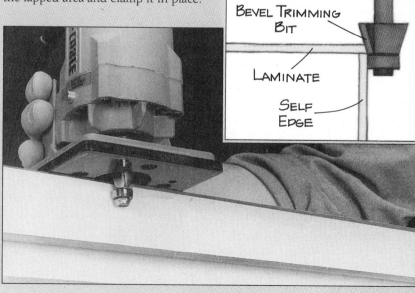

BEVEL TRIMMING BIT — LAMINATE — SELF EDGE

9 **Apply contact cement to the** top surface of the underlayment and the bottom surface of the laminate, and let the cement dry. Place lath strips, dowels, or long, thin scraps of wood over the underlayment, then lay the laminate over the strips. These strips keep the laminate from bonding to the underlayment while you position it.

10 **Once the laminate is** properly positioned above the underlayment, carefully remove the strips one at a time. As you do so, gently press the laminate into place. When all the strips are removed, roll the laminate as you did when applying the self edge. Work from the center of the laminate out toward the edge so you don't leave bubbles or air pockets between the laminate and underlayment.

12 **If the countertop will** have a backsplash, cover the front surface with laminate, then the top surface. (Once again, you don't want liquids to seep into the seam.) Do this *before* you attach the backsplash to the wall. After applying and trimming the laminate, install the backsplash with construction adhesive. If necessary, seal the seam between the backsplash and the countertop with epoxy or latex caulk. **Note:** You can purchase special colored epoxies and caulks to match popular colors of laminates.

(continued) ▷

WORKING WITH LAMINATES — CONTINUED

13 **If the surface you're** covering will have an opening (such as a cutout for a sink or tile inlay), cut or rout the opening *before* applying the laminate. Cover the surface — including the opening — with a single solid sheet. Do *not* attempt to cut an opening in the plastic laminate before you apply it.

14 **After applying the** laminate over the opening, drill a small "starter hole" in the laminate near the center of the opening. Using a flush trim bit, cut out the opening in the laminate, trimming it flush. **Note:** If you rough out the opening in the laminate before you apply it or cut the opening in both the laminate and underlayment after the materials are bonded, you may break or chip the laminate.

PROJECT

6

PUTTING IT ALL TOGETHER: A CABINETRY PROJECT

Few home workshop projects are as large in scope as kitchen cabinets. They are an ambitious project by any stretch of the imagination, requiring many different tasks to bring them all together. They are, however, a completely feasible project for a home craftsman. They don't require expensive tools or special skills, just a modestly equipped shop and plenty of patience and determination.

The story is the same for any built-in cabinet project. Although this chapter describes how to make kitchen cabinets, *the techniques are applicable to any built-in cabinet project* — a bathroom vanity, an entertainment center, workshop storage, or whatever built-in you have in mind. A cabinet design may seem daunting, but the actual construction is not particularly demanding once you get going.

This particular project began, as all major home improvements do, with years of procrastination. My wife, Mary Jane, and I were cursed with a miserable little L-shaped kitchen and less than 8 square feet of counter space. With a few favorite appliances and cookbooks on the counter, there was barely room to open a can of soup. We endured this situation for too long, then decided one day to stop complaining and build something better.

We sketched possible floor plans for new cabinet systems and kept them on the kitchen table, along with several books on kitchen design. For several months, we'd look over the floor plans and books at mealtimes, discussing the advantages of each layout. We narrowed the possibilities down to a U-shaped kitchen with traditional cabinets. I figured the type and number of units needed for the installation, and Mary Jane drew a detailed elevation for each side of the U.

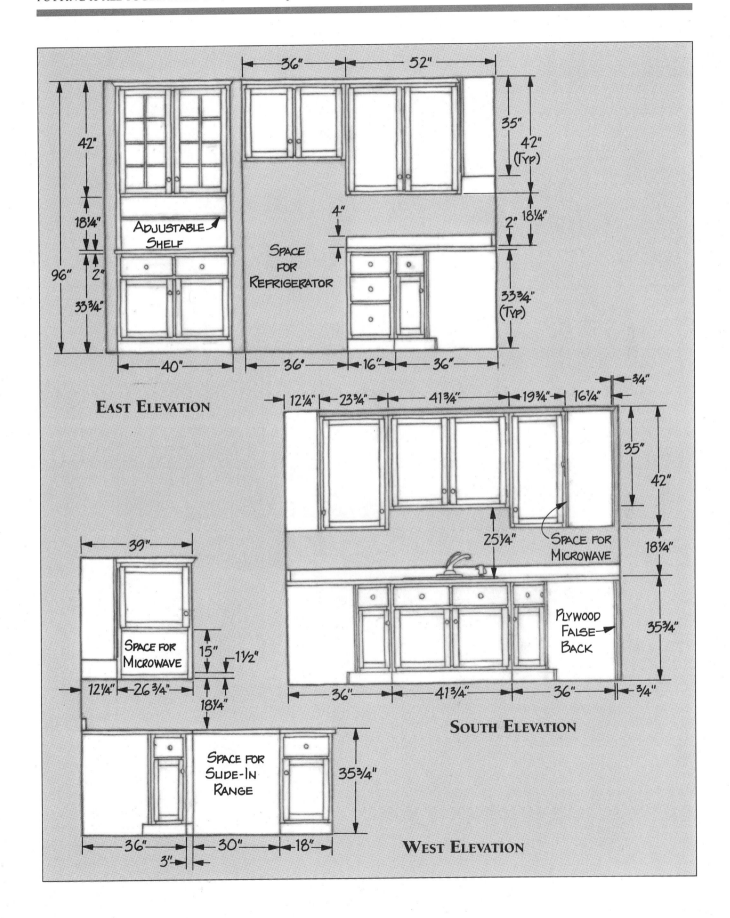

EAST ELEVATION

SOUTH ELEVATION

WEST ELEVATION

WALL UNITS

The new installation required six wall units, each stretching all the way to the ceiling. Most wall units stop 10 to 12 inches below the ceiling — it's difficult for most people to reach a shelf above that level. This unused space often is filled with *soffets,* boxes framed with construction lumber and covered with paneling or drywall. Soffets can be used to hide electrical wiring, recessed lighting, or ventilation ducts. However, we needed the extra storage space that the tall cabinets afforded, even though we wouldn't be able to reach the highest shelves without a stepstool.

Two of the wall units are significantly deeper than the others. The unit over the refrigerator is as deep as the refrigerator itself. If you put a shallow cabinet over the refrigerator, you tend to pile items on top of the refrigerator and block the cabinet doors. The other deep unit holds a microwave. Its opening allows a 1-inch gap between the face frame and the microwave sides and top, as recommended by the manufacturer. This gap helps to dissipate heat when using the appliance. Before designing cabinets that will hold electrical appliances or electronic components, check the owner's manuals for requirements to ensure adequate ventilation. Some older microwaves, for example, require a 4-inch clearance.

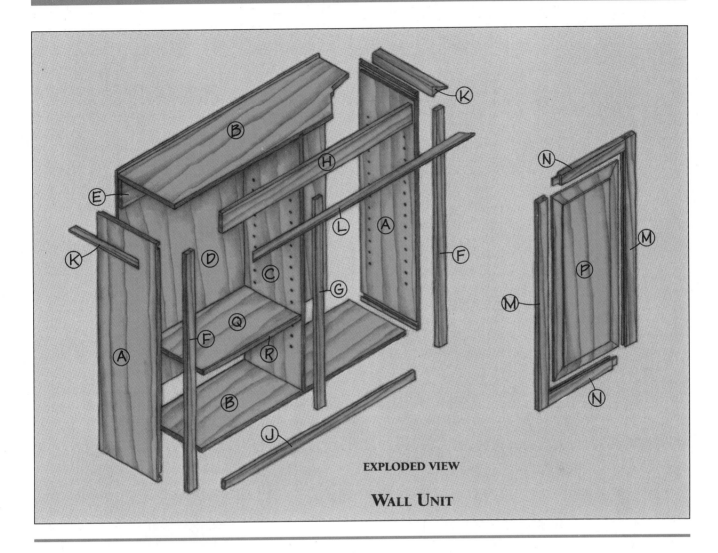

EXPLODED VIEW

WALL UNIT

MATERIALS LIST (FINISHED DIMENSIONS)

Parts

A. Sides* (2) $\frac{3}{4}''$ x $11\frac{1}{2}''$ x 42"

B. Fixed shelves* (2) $\frac{3}{4}''$ x $11\frac{1}{4}''$ x (variable)

C. Divider* (optional) $\frac{3}{4}''$ x $11\frac{1}{4}''$ x $40\frac{3}{4}''$

D. Back* $\frac{1}{4}''$ x (variable) x 42"

E. Nailing strip $\frac{3}{4}''$ x 6" x (variable)

F. Outside face frame stiles (2) $\frac{3}{4}''$ x $1\frac{1}{2}''$ x 42"

G. Middle face frame stile $\frac{3}{4}''$ x $1\frac{1}{2}''$ x 37"

H. Top face frame rail $\frac{3}{4}''$ x $3\frac{1}{2}''$ x (variable)

J. Bottom face frame rail $\frac{3}{4}''$ x $1\frac{1}{2}''$ x (variable)

K. Side moldings (0–2) $1\frac{1}{2}''$ x $1\frac{1}{2}''$ x $13\frac{3}{4}''$

L. Front molding $1\frac{1}{2}''$ x $1\frac{1}{2}''$ x (variable)

M. Door stiles (2 or 4) $\frac{3}{4}''$ x 2" x $37\frac{5}{8}''$

N. Door rails (2 or 4) $\frac{3}{4}''$ x 2" x (variable)

P. Door panels (1 or 2) $\frac{1}{2}''$ x (variable) x $34\frac{1}{4}''$

Q. Adjustable shelves* (2–4) $\frac{3}{4}''$ x $10\frac{7}{8}''$ x (variable)

R. Shelf banding $\frac{1}{4}''$ x $\frac{3}{4}''$ x (variable)

*Make these parts from plywood.

Hardware

#8 x $1\frac{1}{4}''$ Flathead wood screws (36–48)

1" Wire brads (24–36)

4d Finishing nails (12–18)

Semi-concealed self-closing offset hinges and mounting screws (1 or 2 pairs)

Door pulls (1 or 2)

Shelving support pins (8–16)

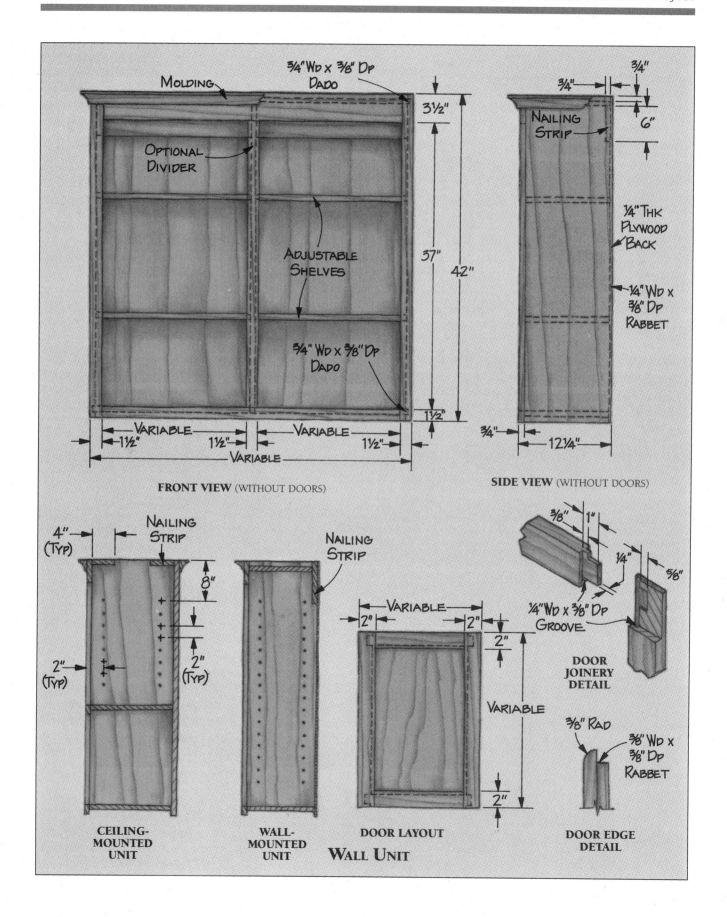

MOLDING

¾" WD x ⅜" DP DADO

OPTIONAL DIVIDER

ADJUSTABLE SHELVES

¾" WD x ⅜" DP DADO

3½"

37"

42"

1½"

VARIABLE
1½"   1½"
VARIABLE
1½"
VARIABLE

FRONT VIEW (WITHOUT DOORS)

¾"   ¾"

6"

NAILING STRIP

¼" THK PLYWOOD BACK

¼" WD x ⅜" DP RABBET

¾"   12¼"

SIDE VIEW (WITHOUT DOORS)

4" (TYP)   NAILING STRIP

8"

2" (TYP)   2" (TYP)

CEILING-MOUNTED UNIT

NAILING STRIP

WALL-MOUNTED UNIT

VARIABLE
2"   2"
2"

VARIABLE

2"

DOOR LAYOUT

WALL UNIT

⅜"   1"

¼"

5/8"

¼" WD x ⅜" DP GROOVE

DOOR JOINERY DETAIL

⅜" RAD

⅜" WD x ⅜" DP RABBET

DOOR EDGE DETAIL

COUNTER UNITS

The installation also required three rectangular counter units, two of which hold one or more drawers. We had originally planned to mount the drawers on metal slides, but when I figured that the hardware for this project would cost nearly $300, we decided to economize by mounting the drawers on wooden web frames with adjustable drawer guides. The web frames were more work than slides, but we shaved over $100 off the hardware bill.

One of the counter units holds the sink. On this unit, we eliminated the web frames and drawer guides to make room for the sink tub. However, we did make drawer faces to cover the top openings in the face frame to make the unit consistent with the others. These drawer faces weren't just for show. We purchased a "sink tray" kit to make two shallow fold-out trays, mounted these trays in the ersatz drawer openings, and attached the drawer faces to them. (The tray hardware is shown on page 15.) These trays hold soap, scrub pads, sponges, and other cleaning paraphernalia that tend to litter the edges of the sink.

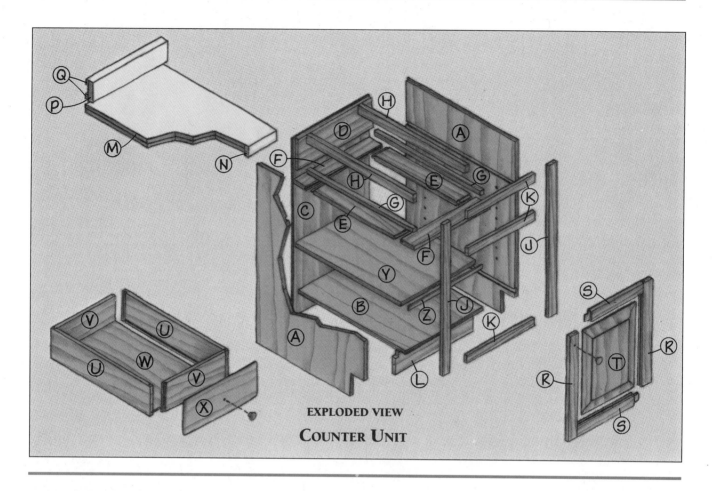

EXPLODED VIEW

COUNTER UNIT

MATERIALS LIST (FINISHED DIMENSIONS)

Parts

A. Sides* (2) $3/4''$ x $23\frac{1}{4}''$ x $34\frac{1}{2}''$

B. Fixed shelf* $3/4''$ x $23''$ x (variable)

C. Back* $1/4''$ x (variable) x $34\frac{1}{2}''$

D. Nailing strip $3/4''$ x $6''$ x (variable)

E. Web frame stiles (2) $3/4''$ x $3''$ x $17\frac{3}{4}''$

F. Web frame rails (2) $3/4''$ x $3''$ x (variable)

G. Drawer guides (2) $1/2''$ x $1/2''$ x $22\frac{1}{4}''$

H. Kickers (2) $3/4''$ x $1\frac{1}{2}''$ x $22\frac{1}{4}''$

J. Face frame stiles (2) $3/4''$ x $1\frac{1}{2}''$ x $30\frac{1}{2}''$

K. Face frame rails (3) $3/4''$ x $1\frac{1}{2}''$ x (variable)

L. Toeboard $3/4''$ x $4\frac{3}{4}''$ x (variable)

M. Counter underlayment† $1\frac{1}{4}''$ x $24\frac{3}{4}''$ x (variable)

N. Counter banding $3/4''$ x $2''$ x (variable)

P. Backsplash† $3/4''$ x $4''$ x (variable)

Q. Spacers (2) $1/2''$ x $1/2''$ x (variable)

R. Door stiles (2) $3/4''$ x $2''$ x $20\frac{5}{8}''$

S. Door rails (2) $3/4''$ x $2''$ x (variable)

T. Door panel $1/2''$ x (variable) x $17\frac{1}{4}''$

U. Drawer sides (2) $1/2''$ x $5\frac{15}{16}''$ x $22\frac{3}{4}''$

V. Drawer front/back (2) $1/2''$ x $5\frac{15}{16}''$ x (variable)

W. Drawer bottom* $1/4''$ x (variable) x $22\frac{1}{4}''$

X. Drawer face $3/8''$ x $6\frac{11}{16}''$ x (variable)

Y. Adjustable shelf* $3/4''$ x $22\frac{5}{8}''$ x (variable)

Z. Shelf banding $1/4''$ x $3/4''$ x (variable)

*Make these parts from plywood.
†Make these parts from particleboard.

Hardware

#8 x $1\frac{1}{4}''$ Flathead wood screws (36–48)

#8 x $1\frac{1}{4}''$ Roundhead wood screws and washers (6)

#8 x $1''$ Flathead wood screws (12–18)

6d Finishing nails (12–18)

1" Wire brads (24–36)

Semi-concealed self-closing offset hinges and mounting screws (1 pair)

Door/drawer pulls (2)

Shelving support pins (4)

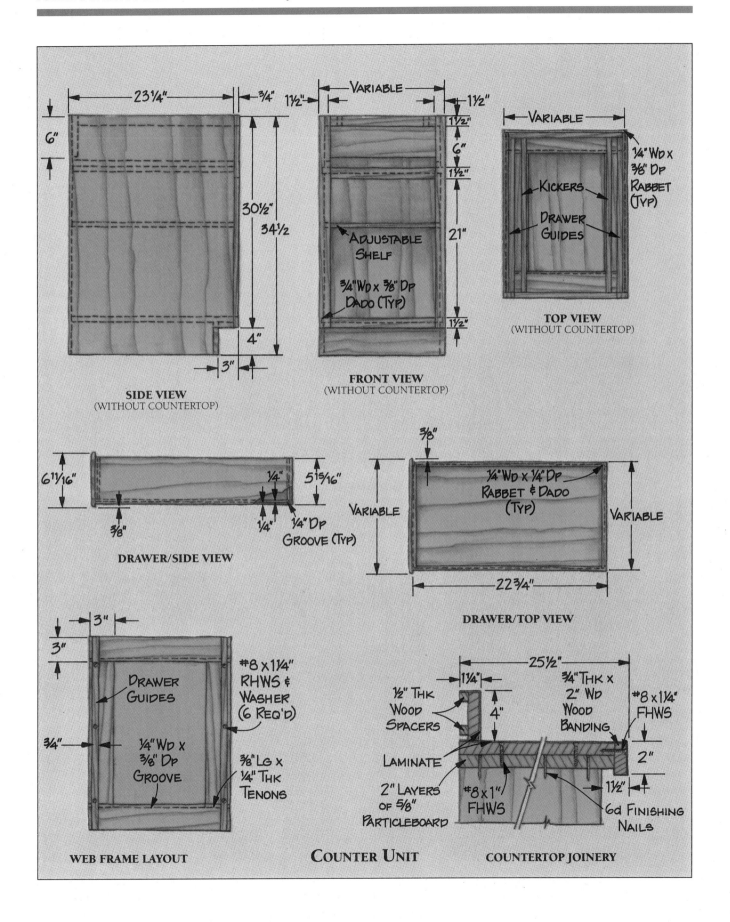

SIDE VIEW
(WITHOUT COUNTERTOP)

FRONT VIEW
(WITHOUT COUNTERTOP)

TOP VIEW
(WITHOUT COUNTERTOP)

DRAWER/SIDE VIEW

DRAWER/TOP VIEW

WEB FRAME LAYOUT

COUNTER UNIT

COUNTERTOP JOINERY

CORNER COUNTER UNITS

Although we turned the corners with the wall units by butting standard rectangular units together, we decided to use two pentagonal corner units for the counter. Because corner counter units are so much broader than standard counter units, this increased the counter space dramatically.

Each corner unit was fitted with revolving shelves and a drawer. While most corner units do not have drawers, we decided to install them to preserve the horizontal line of drawer faces around the kitchen. Aesthetically, this horizontal line ties all the counter cabinets together visually. Practically, it wasted a little storage space — but as precious as storage space is in our kitchen, we thought we could spare a little for good looks.

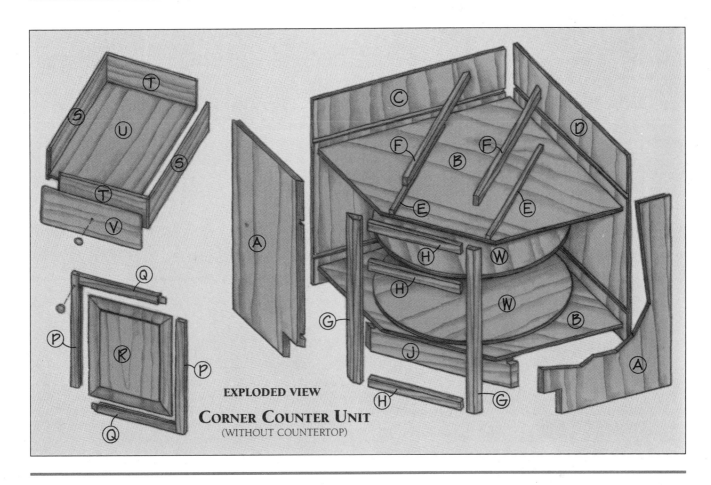

EXPLODED VIEW

Corner Counter Unit
(WITHOUT COUNTERTOP)

Materials List (FINISHED DIMENSIONS)

Parts

A. Sides*
(2) $3/4'' \times 23^{11}/16'' \times 34^{1}/2''$

B. Fixed shelves*
(2) $3/4'' \times 35^{3}/8'' \times 35^{3}/8''$

C. Left back* $1/2'' \times 35^{1}/8'' \times 34^{1}/2''$

D. Right
back* $1/2'' \times 35^{5}/8'' \times 34^{1}/2''$

E. Drawer
guides (2) $1/2'' \times 1/2'' \times 22^{1}/4''$

F. Kickers (2) $3/4'' \times 1^{1}/2'' \times 39^{1}/8''$

G. Face frame
stiles (2) $3/4'' \times 2^{1}/4'' \times 30^{1}/2''$

H. Face frame
rails (3) $3/4'' \times 1^{1}/2'' \times 14''$

J. Toeboard $3/4'' \times 4^{3}/4'' \times 22^{11}/16''$

K. Counter under-
layment† $1^{1}/4'' \times 36'' \times 36''$

L. Counter
banding $3/4'' \times 2'' \times 18''$

M. Backsplash† (2) $3/4'' \times 4'' \times 36''$

N. Spacers (4) $1/2'' \times 1/2'' \times 36''$

P. Door
stiles (2) $3/4'' \times 2'' \times 20^{5}/8''$

Q. Door rails (2) $3/4'' \times 2'' \times 12^{5}/8''$

R. Door
panel $1/2'' \times 11^{1}/4'' \times 17^{1}/4''$

S. Drawer
sides (2) $1/2'' \times 5^{15}/16'' \times 22^{3}/4''$

T. Drawer front/
back (2) $1/2'' \times 5^{15}/16'' \times 13^{7}/16''$

U. Drawer
bottom* $1/4'' \times 13^{7}/16'' \times 22^{1}/4''$

V. Drawer
face $3/8'' \times 6^{11}/16'' \times 14^{11}/16''$

W. Revolving
shelves* (2) $3/4'' \times 33''$ dia.

X. Shelf
banding $1/32'' \times 3/4'' \times 213^{3}/4''$

*Make these parts from plywood.
†Make these parts from particleboard.

Hardware

#8 x 1¼" Flathead wood screws
(36–48)

#8 x 1¼" Roundhead wood
screws and washers (6)

#8 x 1" Flathead wood screws
(12–18)

6d Finishing nails (12–18)

4d Finishing nails (12–18)

Semi-concealed self-closing offset
hinges and mounting screws
(1 pair)

Door/drawer pulls (4)

Carousel hardware and mounting
screws

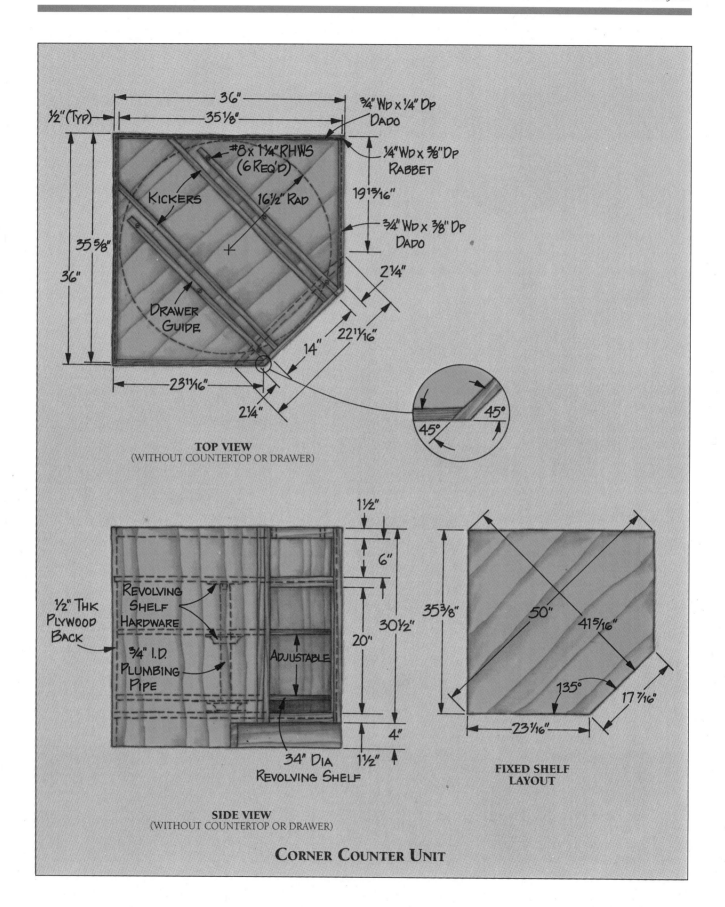

TOP VIEW
(WITHOUT COUNTERTOP OR DRAWER)

SIDE VIEW
(WITHOUT COUNTERTOP OR DRAWER)

**FIXED SHELF
LAYOUT**

CORNER COUNTER UNIT

TALL UNIT

The plans also included one tall unit, which we built in a step-back style. Its doors are glazed with multiple panes to look like an old china cabinet. This unit also has drawers at the same level as the drawers in the counter units. Visually, this helps tie the tall unit to the rest of the system, even though it isn't connected to the other cabinets.

As shown in the drawings, the tall unit is built in one piece. If I had the project to do over again, I would build this unit in two. Originally, we thought that a one-piece unit would look better and be easier to build. We were right — it *was* easier to build. Unfortunately, it was nearly impossible to install. Remember that we decided to extend the cabinets all the way to the ceiling for the extra storage. This prevented me from standing up the tall cabinet until I removed a portion of the ceiling. Then, after the cabinet was installed, I had to repair the ceiling. (Dumb, dumb, dumb…)

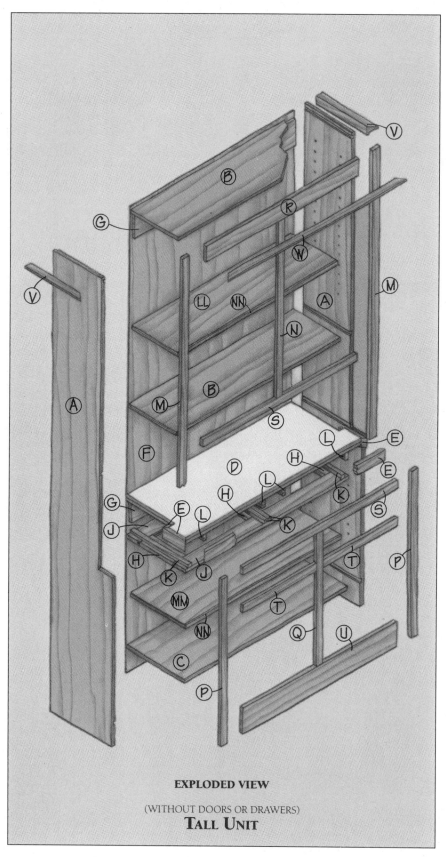

EXPLODED VIEW

(WITHOUT DOORS OR DRAWERS)

TALL UNIT

MATERIALS LIST
(FINISHED DIMENSIONS)

Parts

A. Sides* (2) ³/₄" x 14¹/₄" x 95¹/₂"

B. Top fixed shelves*
(2)   ³/₄" x 11¹/₄" x 39¹/₄"

C. Bottom fixed
shelf*   ³/₄" x 14" x 39¹/₄"

D. Counter† 1¹/₄" x 15³/₄" x 41¹/₂"

E. Counter
banding   ³/₄" x 2" x 62"

F. Back*   ¹/₄" x 39¹/₄" x 95"

G. Nailing
strips (2)   ³/₄" x 6" x 38¹/₂"

H. Web frame
stiles (3)   ³/₄" x 3" x 8³/₄"

J. Web frame
rails (2)   ³/₄" x 3" x 39¹/₄"

K. Drawer
guides (4)   ¹/₂" x ¹/₂" x 14"

L. Kickers (4) ³/₄" x 1¹/₂" x 13¹/₄"

M. Outside top face frame
stiles (2)   ³/₄" x 1¹/₂" x 59¹/₂"

N. Middle top face frame
stile   ³/₄" x 1¹/₂" x 37"

P. Outside bottom face frame
stiles (2)   ³/₄" x 1¹/₂" x 34¹/₂"

Q. Middle bottom face
frame stile ³/₄" x 1¹/₂" x 27¹/₂"

R. Upper top face
frame rail   ³/₄" x 3¹/₂" x 37"

S. Top/bottom face frame
rails (2)   ³/₄" x 1¹/₂" x 37"

T. Middle bottom face frame
rails (2)   ³/₄" x 1¹/₂" x 17³/₄"

U. Lower bottom face
frame rail   ³/₄" x 5¹/₂" x 37"

V. Side moldings
(2)   1¹/₂" x 1¹/₂" x 13³/₄"

W. Front
molding   1¹/₂" x 1¹/₂" x 43"

X. Top door
stiles (4)   ³/₄" x 2" x 37⁵/₈"

Y. Bottom doors
stiles   ³/₄" x 2" x 20⁵/₈"

Z. Door rails (8) ³/₄" x 2" x 15³/₄"

AA. Sash
stiles (2)   ¹/₄" x ¹/₂" x 33⁵/₈"

BB. Sash
rails (12)   ¹/₄" x ¹/₂" x 6¹⁵/₁₆"

CC. Top/bottom vertical glazing
     bars (4) $^3/_{16}"$ x $^1/_2"$ x $8^9/_{16}"$

DD. Middle vertical glazing
     bars (4) $^3/_{16}"$ x $^1/_2"$ x $8^{11}/_{32}"$

EE. Horizontal glazing
     bars (6) $^3/_{16}"$ x $^1/_2"$ x $15^1/_8"$

FF. Door
     panels $^1/_2"$ x $14^3/_8"$ x $17^1/_4"$

GG. Drawer
     sides (4) $^1/_2"$ x $5^{15}/_{16}"$ x 13"

HH. Drawer fronts/
     backs (4) $^1/_2"$ x $5^{15}/_{16}"$ x $17^3/_{16}"$

JJ. Drawer $^1/_4"$ x $12^1/_2"$ x
     bottoms* (2) $17^3/_{16}"$

KK. Drawer
     faces (2) $^3/_8"$ x $6^{11}/_{16}"$ x $18^7/_{16}"$

LL. Top adjustable shelves*
     (2) $^3/_4"$ x $10^7/_8"$ x $38^3/_8"$

MM. Bottom adjustable
     shelf $^3/_4"$ x $13^5/_8"$ x $38^3/_8"$

NN. Shelf
     bandings (3) $^1/_4"$ x $^3/_4"$ x $38^3/_8"$

*Make these parts from plywood.
†Make this part from particleboard.

Hardware

#8 x $1^1/_4"$ Flathead wood screws
  (60–72)

#8 x $1^1/_4"$ Roundhead wood
  screws and washers (12)

1" Wire brads (36–48)

Semi-concealed self-closing offset
  hinges and mounting screws
  (4 pairs)

Door/drawer pulls (4)

Shelving support pins (12)

$^1/_8"$ x $7^3/_8"$ x $8^5/_{16}"$ Glass panes (16)

Glazing points (48)

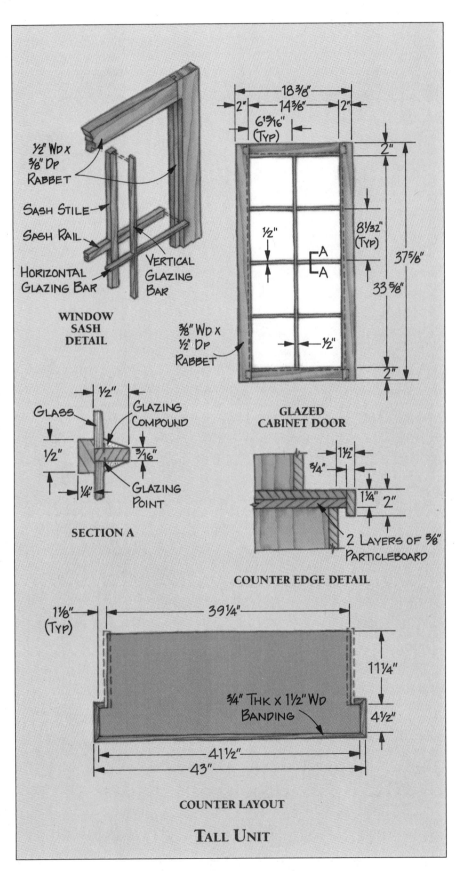

WINDOW
SASH
DETAIL

GLAZED
CABINET DOOR

SECTION A

COUNTER EDGE DETAIL

COUNTER LAYOUT

TALL UNIT

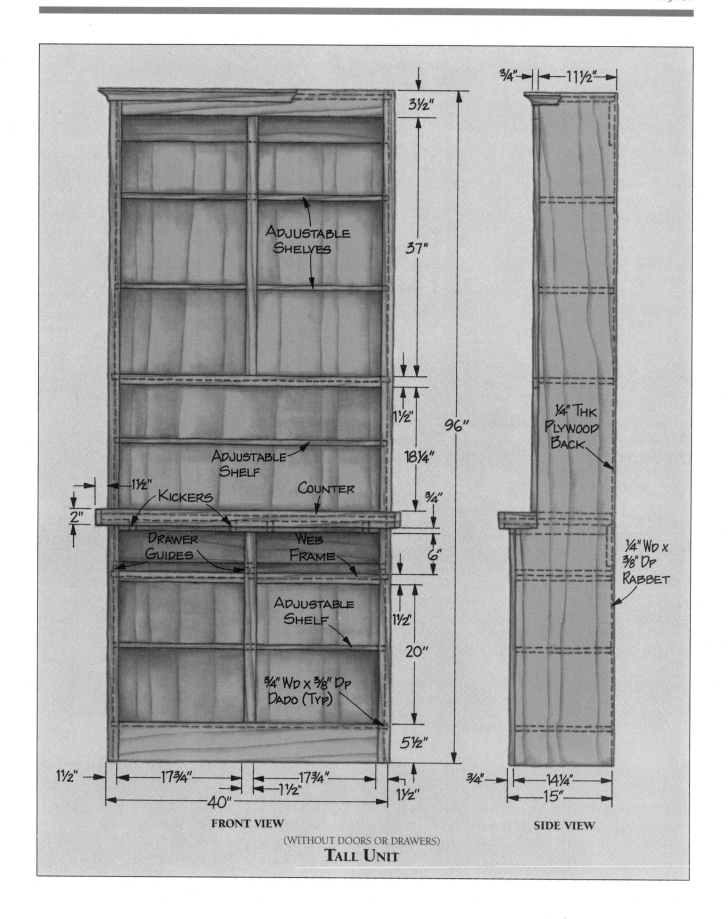

FRONT VIEW

(WITHOUT DOORS OR DRAWERS)

TALL UNIT

SIDE VIEW

PLAN OF PROCEDURE

Note: Although the procedure for making these built-in kitchen cabinets is *generally* the same as for other cabinetry projects, each varies slightly, depending on the design, materials, and installation. Carefully think through the procedures before beginning. You may even wish to list the steps. (If I had thought through all the steps more carefully before jumping into this project, I would have built the tall unit in two sections.)

1 Cut the parts of the cabinet cases to size.

After we finalized the plans and I had a list of materials for each cabinet unit, I figured a cutting list and a shopping list. I purchased the plywood and the hardwood for the cases. As I cut the case parts, I also beveled the edges of the corner unit sides and face frame stiles.

Each part was labeled immediately after being cut so it wouldn't be confused with another. To further prevent a mix-up, I placed the parts for each unit in a separate pile.

TRY THIS TRICK

To make it easier to label the parts, I assigned each cabinet unit a number from 1 through 12. The tall unit, for example, was number 1. When I cut the sides for this unit, I labeled them *1-SIDE*. I wrote these labels on the *ends* or *edges* of the parts because these surfaces would not be sanded before the parts were assembled.

Note: Later on, after all the cases were assembled, I placed them in roughly the same configuration in which I would install them, and asked Mary Jane to take a look. Her first comment was, "Gee, the east wall counter cabinet looks small." I checked the plans and found that in copying the overall dimensions from the elevations to the materials lists, I had mistakenly written down the width of that particular cabinet as 12 inches, when it should have been 16 inches! Even though I double-checked the dimensions on the materials list and the cutting list several times, I never checked either list against the plans! So it was back to step one for that particular unit. (Dumb, dumb, dumb…) Cross-check all your plans and lists to make sure that the dimensions match. Resolve all discrepancies *before* you cut the parts.

2 Cut the joinery in the case parts.

I cut most of the dadoes, rabbets, and grooves needed to assemble the cases with a dado cutter. (*SEE FIGURE 6-1.*) Only the sides of the tall unit, which were too long to cut accurately on a table saw, were dadoed with a router. After setting up the machines to make a particular joint, I retrieved all the parts that required that particular joint from their respective piles, then returned them to the proper piles after cutting the joints. This system was invaluable in keeping track of the parts, but if I had it to do again I would make a cutting list *for the joinery* to help keep track of the joints, too.

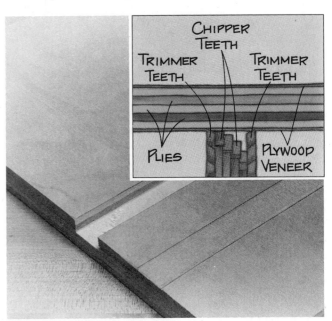

6-1 When cutting dadoes in plywood parts, you must score the joints to prevent the cutter from tearing the veneer. If you use a *stacked* dado, you can use the tool to do this scoring for you. The trimmer blades on most stacked dadoes cut just a little deeper than the chippers. Set the dado cutter to the desired depth of cut, then lower it until only the tips of the trimmer blades protrude above the worktable. Carefully count the revolutions of the depth-of-cut crank as you do this. Turn on the saw and pass the plywood over the cutter, scoring the veneer with the trimmer blades. Then raise the cutter the proper number of revolutions and cut the dado to the full depth.

3 Cut the shapes of the parts. Certain parts needed to be cut to shape — the sides and toeboards of the counter units, the shelves in the corner counter units, and the divider in one wall unit. I used a variety of tools to cut these shapes. Most of them were cut with a band saw or saber saw, but I used the table saw and the *Trimming Guide* (shown on page 50) to cut the pentagonal shelves. The corner counter unit sides and toeboard were cut by hand. (*SEE FIGURE 6-2.*)

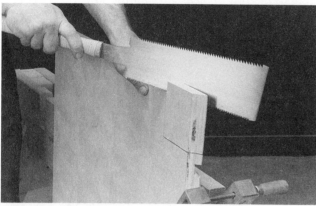

6-2 The edges of the toespace cutouts in the sides of a corner counter unit must be mitered at 45 degrees, and the cutouts in the toe-boards must be mitered to match. I made these angled cutouts with a hand saw, as shown, but you can also use a saber saw by tilting the sole.

6-3 I made the drilling guide for the shelving support holes from two scraps of plywood glued face to face. One end was clearly marked *TOP* and was always aligned with the top layout mark on the part that was being drilled. This ensured that all the holes would line up perfectly.

4 Drill the holes for adjustable shelves. Using a homemade drilling jig, I drilled rows of vertical holes in the sides and dividers. These would hold support pins for the shelves. (*SEE FIGURE 6-3.*)

5 Assemble the standard (rectangular) cases. Once all the parts were fitted, I finish sanded the surfaces of the case parts that would wind up on the *interior* of the cabinets. Then I assembled the rectangular units, joining the parts in this order:
- I glued together the rails and stiles of the web frames.
- After the glue dried, I attached the adjustable drawer guides to the web frames with screws only.
- I also attached kickers to the bottom faces of the top two web frames in the east wall counter unit. This unit would have three drawers stacked one on top of the other.
- I assembled the sides, fixed shelves, and web frames with glue and screws.
- Before the glue that held the shelves to the sides dried, I attached the backs with glue and finishing nails. (*SEE FIGURE 6-4.*)
- I attached the nailing strips to the backs and sides with glue and pocket screws.
- Finally, I attached the topmost kickers to the nailing strips and face frames with glue and pocket screws.

6-4 Attach the back *before* the glue that holds the shelves and web frames in place dries. Adding the back will square the assembly, and all the parts should be properly aligned with one another as the glue dries. I found that most of my cases weren't quite square when I fit the back, so I stretched a long bar clamp diagonally from corner to corner and pulled them square.

6 **Assemble the corner units.** The corner (pentagonal) units had to be assembled in a different sequence than the others:

■ I attached the left backs to the right backs with glue and finishing nails.

■ When the glue dried, I attached the fixed shelves with glue and nails. (*SEE FIGURE 6-5.*)

■ I let the glue dry again, then attached the sides. One side was attached with glue and screws, but the other was attached with screws *only*. I left one side on each of the corner units detachable so I could install the revolving shelves.

Sounds like I thought this one out, right? Actually, in my enthusiasm to put all the cases together, I had dry assembled the corner cabinets in the shop and

was getting ready to glue the parts together, when I noticed two things. The cabinets were too big to get through the kitchen doors, and the openings at the fronts of the cabinets were too small to insert the revolving shelves — dumb mistakes narrowly avoided thanks to good shop procedure.

7 **Install the revolving shelves.** After narrowly avoiding the catastrophe with the corner units, I cut the revolving shelves and banded the edges with veneer. Then I installed the shelves, along with the carousel hardware, in the corner cabinets. (*SEE FIGURE 6-6.*) When the shelves were in place and working properly, I glued the unattached sides to the corner cabinet cases.

6-5 **I found that a corner cabinet** case must be assembled in the reverse of a standard case — first the backs, then the shelves, then the sides.

6-6 **If you install revolving** shelves in a corner cabinet, it helps to mark where you will install the pivots on the fixed shelves *before* you assemble the cabinet. (The pivots must be placed at the center of the revolving shelves.) I drilled 1/8-inch-diameter holes to mark the pivots. That way, I could sand the fixed shelves without worrying about removing the marks.

8 **Assemble the face frames.** On most cabinets, the face frames overhang the sides slightly, creating a fitting allowance. For this reason, I made the face frame rails 1/8 inch longer than specified. The assembled frames protruded 1/16 inch on each side.

The frame members were assembled with glue and pocket screws. I used the "Pocket Hole Jig" shown on page 64 to drill two angled holes in each end of each rail, then fastened the rails to the stiles with 1 1/2-inch-long drywall screws. (*See Figure 6-7.*)

TRY THIS TRICK

Because the frame members are glued end grain to long grain, the glue joints are relatively weak. You can make them a great deal stronger by applying a thin coat of glue to the adjoining ends of the rails, waiting 15 to 30 minutes, then applying a second glue coat just before screwing the rails to the stiles. On most end-grain-to-long-grain glue joints, the glue is absorbed by the end grain before it dries, and the resulting connection is "starved" for glue. Using this technique, the first coat of glue seals the end grain and prevents the second coat from being absorbed.

---

9 **Attach the face frames and toeboards to the cabinet cases.** I centered the frames on the cases so they protruded the same distance from each side, then attached them to the front edges of the cabinets using glue and screws. Then the toeboards were fitted to the cases and fastened in the same manner. I counterbored all the screw holes, then covered the screw heads with wooden plugs.

FOR YOUR INFORMATION

Some cabinetmakers drill small holes (about 3/8 inch in diameter) near the top edges of the toeboards, where they won't be seen on the assembled cabinet. This helps ventilate the space below the bottom shelf.

---

10 **Install the top kickers.** After the face frames were installed, I fastened the kickers for the top drawers between the top face frame rails and the nailing strips, using glue and pocket hole screws. On the corner units, the kickers were fastened directly to the backs.

11 **Cut the parts for the drawers and doors.** When all the cases were assembled, I measured the door and drawer openings and compared the dimensions to those on the plans. Then I measured and compared them again. By this time, I had already made one cabinet case twice because I failed to cross-check my measurements. I was determined not to repeat the same mistake with any of the doors and drawers.

Once I was confident of the measurements, I figured the cutting list for the doors and drawers — and cross-checked the figures on the cutting list. Finally, I cut the parts to size.

12 **Assemble the doors.** I decided to use a haunched mortise-and-tenon joint to assemble the door frames. This is a strong joint and relatively easy to make:
- Cut grooves in the inside edges of all frame members.
- Rout or drill mortises near the ends of the stiles.
- Cut tenons to fit the mortises in the ends of the rails.
- Notch the tenons to create the haunches.

After cutting and fitting the frame members, I finish sanded the door parts and assembled the doors. I glued the tenons in the mortises and as I did so, I slid the panels into their grooves. (*See Figure 6-12.*) I did *not* glue the panels in the frames; I let them float in the grooves.

I also used haunched mortises and tenons to assemble the frames for the glazed doors in the tall unit.

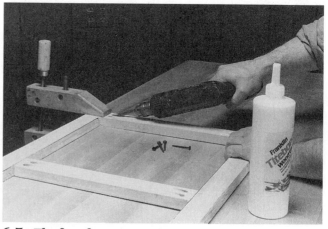

6-7 The face frames were assembled with pocket hole screws. When fastening a rail to a stile, I found it helps to clamp *both* parts to the workbench, as shown. This held them in place while I drove the screws.

After assembling the rails and stiles, I let the glue dry thoroughly and routed the inside edge of the frame, widening the groove to make a rabbet. Then I glued the sash work in the rabbet, creating frames for the small panes of glass. (SEE FIGURE 6-8.)

After assembling the doors, I rabbeted the outside edges to create the lips, then rounded-over the lips.

13 Assemble the drawers.

I assembled the drawer parts with simple dadoes, rabbets, and grooves:

■ The inside faces of the drawer fronts, backs, and sides were dadoed to hold the drawer bottoms.

■ The sides were dadoed to hold the fronts and backs.

■ The ends of the fronts and backs were rabbeted to fit the side dadoes. I also rounded-over the edges of the drawer faces.

After finish sanding the drawer parts, I glued the fronts, backs, and sides together. While putting these parts together, I slid the drawer bottoms into their grooves, but I did *not* glue the bottoms in place. After letting the drawer assemblies dry, I glued the faces to the drawer fronts.

14 Install the doors and drawers.

Both the doors and drawers were built as close as possible to their *final* dimensions — slightly undersize for their openings. Because these assemblies were lipped, I did not feel it was necessary to build them oversize and then shave them to fit. Even so, some of the completed doors and drawers were snug in their openings. If a door was snug, I shaved the shoulders of the outside rabbet with a bullnose plane. (SEE FIGURE 6-9.) If a drawer was too big, I sanded the surfaces that rubbed in the case with a random-orbit sander.

When the doors fit properly, I mounted hinges on the appropriate stiles. I laid the cabinets on their backs, put the doors in place, and screwed the hinges to the face frames. To install the drawers, the guides were adjusted side to side until the drawers slid smoothly in and out of the cabinets with a minimum of slop. I also installed pulls on the doors and drawers.

15 Make the adjustable shelves.

After sitting down and listing what we planned to store in each unit, Mary Jane and I decided how many adjustable shelves we needed for each unit with cupboard space. I carefully measured — and re-measured — the insides of the units, then cut the shelves from plywood. I made each shelf 1/8 inch narrower (side to side) and 3/8 inch shallower (front to back) than the space it would occupy. I glued a 1/4-inch thick strip of hardwood to the front edge of the adjustable shelf to hide the plies. This made the shelves 1/8 inch smaller than the interior width and depth of the cabinet.

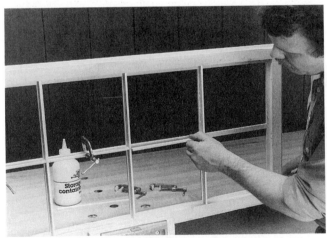

6-8 To install the sash work in the glazed doors, I had to rout a rabbet in the inside edges of the assembled door frames. I squared the corners of this rabbet with a chisel, then glued the sash frame members in place in this order: (1) horizontal glazing bars, (2) sash stiles, (3) sash rails, and finally (4) vertical glazing bars. In assembling these pieces, I clamped each part in place, let the glue set up, then removed the clamps and fastened the next part.

6-9 To fit the lipped doors, I shaved the outside rabbets with a bullnose plane. This enlarged the lips without changing the outside dimensions of the doors.

16 **Apply the first coat of finish.** Once I built all the cabinet units, I removed all the doors and drawers and all the hardware (except for the revolving shelves), and sanded those surfaces that still required it. Then I painted *all* the wood surfaces — inside and out — with white primer. With the insides of the cabinets painted, they would be easier to clean. (*SEE FIGURE 6-10.*)

Note: Had my wife and I elected to apply a stain or a clear finish, I might have decided to complete the finishing job at this point. After all, most commercially made cabinets are installed that way. But I figured the white paint might get scuffed or dirty during the installation, and it would be better to complete the paint job after the cabinets were installed. Later events showed that this was a wise decision.

17 **Remove the old cabinets and mark the studs.** Once the cabinets units were built, we faced the next challenge — installation. And in order to install the new cabinets, we had to rip the old ones out.

As the old cabinets came down, I paid close attention to where they had been attached. The old screw holes helped show where most of the studs were in the walls. I quickly found the remaining studs with the tap-and-drill method described on page 82 and marked them with drafting tape. (*SEE FIGURE 6-11.*)

18 **Run new wiring and plumbing.** The best time to run new wiring and plumbing is when you can easily reach the walls. Our installation required several new electrical circuits and a small addition to the water pipes. I removed a portion of the drywall so the electrician and plumber could easily run lines inside the walls, then patched it after the work was done. **Note:** Because changes in the electrical and plumbing service must meet local standards, it's best to have this work done by professionals who are familiar with the codes.

19 **Add a false back.** The west cabinets form a peninsula that juts out from the south wall. To face the back of this peninsula, I installed a false back — a sheet of 3/4-inch plywood that was as long as the planned peninsula and as tall as the counter units. (*SEE FIGURE 6-12.*)

20 **Install the counter units and tall unit.** When the space had been prepared for the cabinets, I scooted the counter units in place. As I did so, I drilled access holes in a counter unit for plumbing pipes, and in a corner unit for the electrical line to the stove.

I tried leveling the units one at a time, but found it tedious. So I clamped most of the counter units together with the top edges flush and leveled the entire assembly. Once the units were level, I fastened

6-10 **Here's what our kitchen** cabinet project looked like halfway to the finish line. All the cases are built, the doors and drawers are fitted, and the first coat of paint is dry.

them together with wood screws, then fastened them to the wall with lag screws.

The tall unit probably would have been the simplest of all the units to install had it been built in two sections. But it proved to be too tall to stand up. (Actually, it was half an inch short of the ceiling, but the *diagonal* measurement from the top rear corner to the bottom front corner was a full inch taller.) After considering all the options for two weeks, I finally decided to cut a slot in the ceiling so I could stand the unit up and slide it in place. Once this was done, it was an easy matter to level it and fasten it to the wall. Later, I repaired the hole in the ceiling with drywall and spackle.

21 Attach the underlayment and banding to the counter units.
I carefully measured the installed corner cabinet, then cut the parts of the particleboard underlayment to size. I made this underlay-

6-11 Once I found the studs in the walls, I marked their locations with chalk and a snap line. To make each line, I drove a finishing nail partway into the stud near the ceiling, then hooked the end of the snap line to the nail. I drove a second nail into the stud near the floor, stretched the line taut between the nails, and snapped the string against the wall. This left a straight chalk line. **Note:** I used *blue* chalk to snap the line. Blue chalk washes off the wall easily, while red is more tenacious and bleeds through the paint.

ment from two sheets of 5/8-inch particleboard. I nailed the bottom sheet directly to the top edges of the counter cabinets then attached the top sheet to it with screws. This arrangement makes the countertop fairly easy to remove, should it ever be necessary — just pull it straight up.

With the underlayment secured, I faced the front edge with hardwood banding. I fastened this banding to the underlayment with glue and screws. I countersunk all the screws in the underlayment and banding so the heads were flush with the surface. (*SEE FIGURE 6-13.*)

Note: I set the heads of the nails so they were level with the underlayment or banding surface, but I did not attempt to hide them because the plastic laminate would cover them. If, for some reason, you feel you might want to remove or replace the countertop, attach it from below with cleats or pocket screws and don't cover the heads of the screws.

22 Hang the wall cabinets.
Unlike the counter cabinets, the wall cabinets were hung one at a time. I started with the east wall cabinet that hung over the refrigerator. Since there was no counter below this unit, I suspended it on deadmen. I set the other east wall unit on the counter next to it, just to make sure that both units would fit in the space allotted. Then I drove lag screws through the nailing strip and into the studs in the east wall. For good measure, I also drove a lag screw through the side of the cabinet and into the north wall.

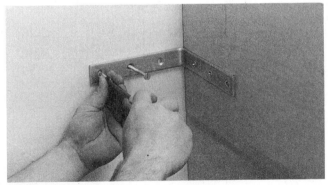

6-12 While we planned to attach the east and south cabinets to walls, the western portion of the system was designed as a freestanding peninsula. To create a back for this peninsula, I attached one end of a sheet of plywood to the south wall with metal brackets. I banded the unattached end of the plywood with a 1/4-inch-thick strip of hardwood to hide the plies.

Then I installed the adjoining units in order, resting each one on support blocks to position it. I screwed each wall unit to the wall *and* the preceding cabinet. The last cabinet to be installed — the west wall unit, which holds the microwave — had to be attached to the ceiling, since there was no wall behind it. Unfortunately, when the cabinet was positioned, the nailing strips were parallel to and nowhere near the ceiling joists. So I crawled up in the attic and nailed several stringers between the joists that straddled the west wall unit. Then I screwed the cabinet to these stringers.

23 **Cut the hole for the sink.** Using the sink trim (the metal band that goes around the installed sink) as a template, I laid out the necessary hole in the countertop. I drilled a 1-inch-diameter hole in the waste to start the cutout, then completed it with a saber saw. (SEE FIGURE 6-14.)

24 **Install the laminate.** I attached the self edge to the countertop banding, trimmed it, then covered the underlayment with laminate. (SEE FIGURE 6-15.) Before gluing the large sheets of plastic laminate to the countertop, I cut them slightly oversize and jointed the edges where they met. There were two long joints over the corner cabinets.

25 **Attach the backsplashes.** Although I did not fit the underlayment (or the laminate that covered it) to the wall, I did fit the backsplashes. Next, these were covered with plastic laminate. Then the laminated backsplashes were glued to the wall with construction adhesive. There were a few small gaps between the backsplashes and the countertop and between the wall and the backsplashes, but I filled these in with a latex caulk that matched the wood tones in the laminate.

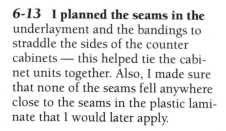

6-13 I planned the seams in the underlayment and the bandings to straddle the sides of the counter cabinets — this helped tie the cabinet units together. Also, I made sure that none of the seams fell anywhere close to the seams in the plastic laminate that I would later apply.

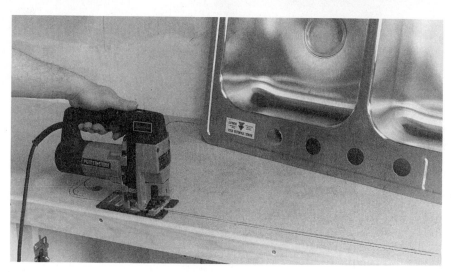

6-14 It's best to make the sink cutout *after* you hang the wall cabinets. If you do things the other way around, it's difficult to support the cabinet over the sink while you install it.

26 **Attach the trim and other finishing touches.** I covered the back of the west wall unit (which hung so the side was against the wall) with thin tongue-and-groove paneling. I also paneled the plywood false back that covered the backs of the west counter units to match it. Then I attached molding around the tops of the wall units and tall unit, and along the base of the false back. (*SEE FIGURE 6-16.*)

27 **Finish the cabinets.** With all the cabinets installed and trimmed, I installed the glass panes in the glazed doors for the tall unit. Mary Jane and I applied another coat of paint to all the accessible wood surfaces on all the cabinets, inside and out. We also painted the doors and drawer faces. After the paint dried, we replaced the doors and drawers in the cabinets.

6-15 Covering the countertop required several broad sheets of plastic laminate. I cut these oversize, jointed the adjoining edges, then kept all the sheets in place with masking tape. I glued this entire assembly down in one step, as if it were a single sheet.

6-16 We used molding to hide any gaps between the tops of the wall units and the ceiling. I attached it with glue and finishing nails and set the heads of the nails. Later, I covered the nail heads with wood putty and painted the molding.

A Parting Thought

And that was that! Was it worth the trouble? The kitchen is a joy to work in — just having the additional counterspace is adequate compensation for all our work. Would we do it all over again? Yes and no. I wouldn't hesitate to tackle a large cabinetry project, but I might proceed differently. I have since talked to two craftsmen who planned their own kitchens so they could install the cabinets in stages. They built one or two units at a time, removed a *portion* of the old cabinets, and installed the new ones in their place. They continued in this manner until they had a new kitchen. In one instance, the entire project took over two years, but the gentleman who built it told me "it never *felt* like a large project" because he tackled one small piece at a time. This procedure works well not only for kitchen cabinets, but also for other large built-in cabinet systems. If the project seems too ambitious, cut it down to size by dividing it into *several* projects.

INDEX

Note: Page references in *italic* indicate photographs or illustrations.
Boldface references indicate charts or tables.

A

Adjustable router guide, 61, *61, 62, 63*

B

Backsplash, 88-90, *90, 95,* 120
Banding, 58, *58,* 59, *59,* 89, *90,* 119
Biscuit joint, 55, *55, 56*
Bottom supports, *29*
Bridle joint, *71*
Butcherblock, *86, 90*
Butt hinge, 72, *73*

C

Cabinet styles
  contemporary, 12, *12,* 23, 24
  traditional, 12, *12,* 23, 24
Carousels, 34
Case construction
  assembly, 59, 60, *60,* 114, *114,* 115,
    115, 116
  back, 23, *23,* 27, 114, *114,* 118
  cleats, 29
  corner counter unit, 3, *3, 4,* 9, **10,**
    11, 33, *33,* 106, *106-108, 114,*
    115, *115*
  counter unit, 3, *3,* 8, **10,** *11,* 29, *29,*
    31, 83, *84,* 103, *103-105,* 119
  cutting parts, 113, 114
  dividers, 23, 27
  drawer support, *29*
  face frame, 23, *23,* 33, 55, *55-57*
  nailing strip, 23, *23,* 27, *27,* 28, 32,
    33
  shelves, 23, *26,* 27, 28, 53, 69
  sides, 23
  tall unit, 3, *3,* 8, *8,* **10,** *10,* 32, *32,*
    109, *109-112*
  toeboard, 23, *31, 33,* 116
  toespace, *114*
  wall unit, 3, *3,* 8, **10,** 11, *11,* 27, *27,*
    28, 100, *100-102*
Ceramic tile, 87, *87*
Circular saw guide, 45, *46, 47, 49*

Cleats, 23, *29, 90*
Corian, 85, *86*
Corner counter unit
  assembly, 115, *115*
  construction, 33, *33*
  dimensions, 9, **10,** *11*
  nailing strip, *33*
  pentagonal cross section, 3, *4, 33*
  plans, 106, *106-108*
  toeboard, *33*
  toespace, *114*
Counter unit
  banding, 119
  bottom supports, *29*
  construction, 3, *3,* 29, *29, 31*
  dimensions, 8, **10,** *11*
  installation, 118
  free-standing, *31*
  shims, 83, *84*
  installation, 80, 81, *81, 82,* 83, *83,*
    84
  plans, 103, *103-105*
  toespace, 29, *29, 31*
Countertop
  backsplash, 88-90, *90, 95,* 120
  banding, 58, *58,* 59, *59,* 89, *90,* 119
  installation, 85, *86,* 87, *87,* 88-90,
    90, 96
Countertop materials
  butcherblock, *86, 90*
  ceramic tile, 87, *87*
  Corian, 85, *86*
  fiberboard, 85, *86*
  laminate, 85, *86, 90*
  metal, 87, *87*
  solid wood, 85, *86*
  stone, 87, *87*
  underlayment, 88, *90, 90,* 119, *120*
Cutting grid, 40, *40,* 45, *45, 47-49*

D

Dado, 44, 53, *53, 54, 62, 63,* 113, *113*
Dado cutter, 44, 52, *52, 53*
Dado shims, 52, *52*

Deadmen, 83, *85,* 88, *89*
Dimensions
  corner wall unit, 9, **10,** *11*
  corner counter unit, 9, **10**
  counter unit, 8, **10,** *11*
  doors, 9, **10,** *71*
  drawers, 9, **10**
  shelves, 9, **10**
  tall unit, 8, *8,* **10,** 10
  wall unit, 8, **10,** *11*
Door(s)
  assembly, 116
  board-and-batten, 26, *26, 70*
  bridle joint, *71*
  cutting parts for, 69, 116
  dimensions, 9, **10,** *71*
  dowels, *71*
  frame-and-panel, 26, *26,* 70, *70,*
    101, 102, 104
  glazed, *111,* 117
  hanging, 72, *73,* 74, *74*
  hardware, 72, *73,* 74, *74*
  hinge mortise for, *73*
  inset, 23, *24,* 70
  installation, 117
  lipped, 23, *25,* 70, 117
  overlay, 23, *25,* 70
  sash joint, 72, *111,* 117
  slab, 26, *26,* 70
Doweling jig, 56
Dowels, 55, *55, 56, 71*
Drawer(s)
  assembly, *104, 105, 107,* 117
  binding or rubbing, 78
  brackets, *30,* 57, *57*
  cutting parts for, 69, 116
  dimensions, 9, **10**
  face, 75
  half-blind dovetail, 76, *76*
  hardware, *30,* 57, *57*
  inset, *24,* 77, *77*
  installation, 75, 77, *77,* 78, *78,* 117
  kickers, *30,* 116
  lipped, 23, *25,* 75, *77*
  lock joint, 76, *76*

overlay, 23, 25, 75
rails, *54*
stiles, *54*
slides, *30*
supports, *29*
web frame, *30, 54, 105*
Drawer brackets, *30, 57, 57*
Drawer supports, *29*
Drawer slides, *77, 78*
Drill guide, *79, 114*

E

Estimating materials
    cutting list, 17, *17, 18*
    list of materials, 17, 18, *18*
Euro-hinge, 72, 74, *74*

F

Face frame, 23, *23, 33, 55, 55-57,*
    116, *116*
Fiberboard, 85, *86*
Finishing touches, 118, 121, *121*
Fitting allowance, 35, *35, 36*
Flush trim router base, *58, 68, 68*

G

Groove, 44, *53, 54, 62*

H

Half-blind dovetail, 76, *76*
Hardware
    butt hinge, 72, *73*
    drawer brackets, *30, 57, 57*
    Euro-hinge, 72, 74, *74*
    standards and clips, 78, *79*
    support pins, 78, *78*
    surface-mount hinge, 72, *73*
    wire supports, 79, *79*
    wrap-around hinge, 72
Haunched mortise and tenon, 72
Hinge mortise, *73*

J

Joinery
    biscuit, 55, *55, 56*
    bridle joint, *71*
    dado, 44, *53, 53, 54, 62, 63,* 113,
        113
    half-blind dovetail, 76, *76*
    dowel, 55, *55, 56, 71*
    groove, 44, *53, 54, 62*
    haunched mortise and tenon, 72
    hinge mortise, *73*

lap joint, 55, *55, 56*
lock joint, 76, *76*
pocket screw, 55, *55, 57,* 64, *65, 90,*
    116
rabbet, 44, 53, *53, 54, 75, 75*
sash joint, 72, *117*

K

Kickers, *30,* 116
Kitchen design
    cabinets, 19
    galley, *20*
    island, *21, 29*
    L-shaped, *21*
    major appliances, 19
    microwave, 19
    peninsula, 29
    sink, 19
    stove, 19
    strip, *20*
    U-shaped, *6, 16, 20*
    work centers, 19
    work triangle, 19

L

Laminate
    as countertop material, 85, *86, 90*
    cutting guide, 91, *91, 92, 94*
    installation, *86,* 91, *92-96,* 120, *121*
    sink cutout, *96*
    trimming, *92, 93, 94*
Laminate cutting guide, 91, *91, 92, 94*
Lap joint, 55, *55, 56*
Lock joint, 76, *76*

M

Mounting strips, 27, *28*
Mullions, 27

N

Nailing strip, 23, *23,* 27, *27, 28, 32, 33*

P

Particleboard, 37, 38, *38*
    circular saw guide, 45, *46, 47, 49*
    cutting, 40, *40,* 41, *41,* 42, *42,* 43,
        43, 44, *44,* 45, *45, 46, 47,* 52, *52*
    cutting aids, 45, *45-51*
    cutting grid, 40, *40,* 45, *45, 47-49*
    handling and support, 40, *40,* 45, *45*
    layout 41, *41*
    trimming guide, 43, *43, 44,* 45, *46,*
        47, 50, 51

Pentagonal cross section, 3, *4, 33*
Planning
    cutting list, 17, *17,* 18
    design, 2, *5-7,* 8, 9, **10,** 12, *12,* 14,
        15, 16, 19, *20, 21,* 23, *24,* 29
    layout, 16, *16*
    list of materials, 17, 18, *18*
Plywood, 37
    circular saw guide, 45, *46, 47, 49*
    cutting, 40, *40,* 41, *41,* 42, *42,* 43,
        43, 44, *44,* 45, *45, 46, 47,* 52, *52*
    cutting aids, 45, *45-51*
    cutting grid, 40, *40,* 45, *45, 47-49*
    handling and support, 40, *40,* 45, *45*
    layout, 41, *41*
    trimming guide, 43, *43, 44,* 45, *46,*
        47, 50, 51
Plywood cutting grid, 40, *40,* 45, *45,*
    47-49, 92
Pocket hole jig, 64, *64-67*
Pocket screw, 55, *55, 57,* 64, *65, 90,*
    116
Projects
    corner counter unit, 106, *106-108*
    counter unit, 103, *103-105*
    tall unit, 109, *109-112*
    wall unit, 100, *100-102*

R

Rabbet, 44, 53, *53, 54, 75, 75*
Rails, 27, *54*
Rectangular cross section, 3, *3*

S

Sash joint, 72, *111, 117*
Scribe strip, 14, *14, 35*
Shelves
    adjustable, 27, *28,* 78, *78,* 114, *114*
    construction of, 117
    corner unit, 115, *115*
    dimensions, 9, *9,* **10**
    drilling holes for, 114, *114*
    fixed, *23,* 27, *28, 53,* 115
    half-round, *15*
    hardware, 78, *78,* 79
    installation, 53, 78, *78,* 115, *115*
    middle, *23, 32, 33*
    open, *26*
    revolving, 115, *115*
Shims, 83, *84*
Sink cutout, *96,* 120, *120*
Standards and clips, 78, *79*
Stiles, 27, *54*
Story stick, 13, *13,* 14
Studs, locating, 81, *82,* 118, *119*

Support blocks, 88, *88*
Support pins, 78, *78*
Surface-mount hinge, 72, *73*

T

Tall unit
   chimney style, *8*
   construction, 3, *3,* 32, *32*
   dimensions, 8, **10,** *10*
   hutch style, *8*
   installation, 118
   middle shelves, *32*
   nailing strips, *32*
   plans, 109, *109-112*
   step-back style, *8*
   ventilation, *33*
Toeboard, *23, 31, 33,* 116
Toespace, 29, *29, 31, 114*
Trimming guide, 43, *43, 44,* 45, *46,*
   47, 50, 51

U

U-shaped jig, *56*
Underlayment, 88, 90, *90,* 119, *120*

V

Ventilation, *33*

W

Wall unit
   construction, 3, *3,* 27, *27, 28*
   corner dimensions, 9, **10,** *11*
   dimensions, 8, **10,** *11*
   installation, 85, *85,* 88, *88, 89,* 119
   plans, 100, *100-102*
   mounting strips, 27, *28*
   mullions, *27*
   nailing strip, 27, *27, 28*
   rails, *27*
   soffet, 100
   stiles, *27*
   support blocks, 88, *88*
Web frame, *30,* 54, *54,* 55, *105*
Wire supports, 79, *79*
Wiring and plumbing, 118
Wobble dado, *52*
Work centers
   food preparation, 19
   mixing, 19
   serving, 19
Work triangle, 19
Workshop cabinet, *5, 86*
Wrap-around hinge, 72

WOODWORKING GLOSSARY

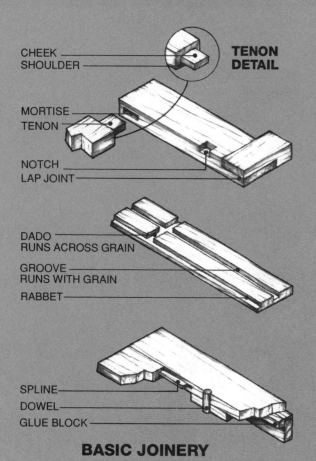

TENON DETAIL
- CHEEK
- SHOULDER

- MORTISE
- TENON
- NOTCH
- LAP JOINT

- DADO RUNS ACROSS GRAIN
- GROOVE RUNS WITH GRAIN
- RABBET

BASIC JOINERY
- SPLINE
- DOWEL
- GLUE BLOCK

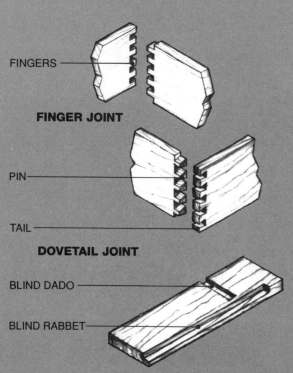

FINGER JOINT
- FINGERS

DOVETAIL JOINT
- PIN
- TAIL

SPECIAL JOINERY
- BLIND DADO
- BLIND RABBET

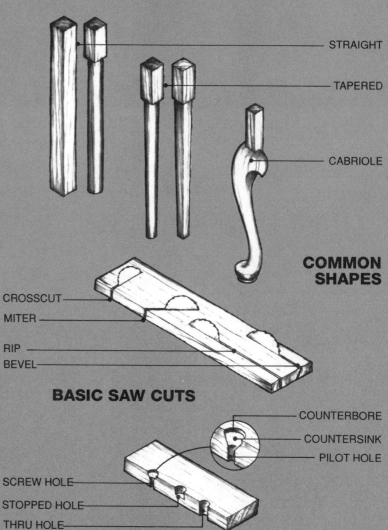

COMMON SHAPES
- STRAIGHT
- TAPERED
- CABRIOLE

BASIC SAW CUTS
- CROSSCUT
- MITER
- RIP
- BEVEL

HOLES
- COUNTERBORE
- COUNTERSINK
- PILOT HOLE
- SCREW HOLE
- STOPPED HOLE
- THRU HOLE

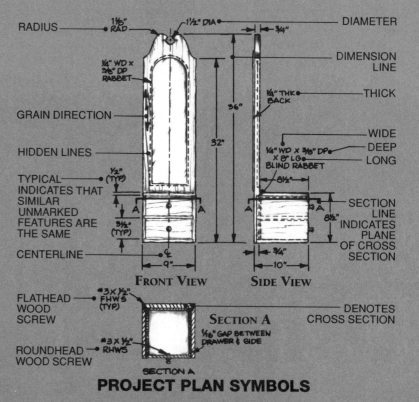

- RADIUS — 1⅛" RAD
- 1½" DIA
- ¾"
- DIAMETER
- ¼" WD X ⅜" DP RABBET
- DIMENSION LINE
- 36"
- ¼" THK BACK — THICK
- GRAIN DIRECTION
- 32"
- ¼" WD X ⅜" DP X 8" LG BLIND RABBET — WIDE / DEEP / LONG
- HIDDEN LINES
- TYPICAL INDICATES THAT SIMILAR UNMARKED FEATURES ARE THE SAME — ½" (TYP)
- 8½"
- 3½" (TYP)
- A A
- SECTION LINE INDICATES PLANE OF CROSS SECTION
- 8½"
- CENTERLINE
- ℄
- 9"
- ¾"
- 10"
- **FRONT VIEW**
- **SIDE VIEW**

- FLATHEAD WOOD SCREW — #3 X ½" FHWS (TYP)
- **SECTION A**
- 1/16" GAP BETWEEN DRAWER & SIDE
- DENOTES CROSS SECTION
- ROUNDHEAD WOOD SCREW — #3 X ½" RHWS
- SECTION A

PROJECT PLAN SYMBOLS